The Wobbit A Parody
(Of Tolkien's <u>The Hobbit</u>)

or
There Goes My Back Again

by Paul A. Erickson

This book is dedicated to Mary Beth, for saying "yes" to the project, time after time.

CONTENTS

CHAPTER		PAGE
1	An Unexpected Brunch	5
2	Mutton Roast, $2.95 lb.	21
3	Rest Stop — 2 Miles	35
4	Over Hill, Over Dale	44
5	Riddles With A Dork	54
6	I Ordered My Entrée Fried, Not Broiled	66
7	Queer Lodgings For The Straight Wobbit	78
8	Guys Versus Spiders	92
9	Beer Barrel Bondage	110
10	Happiness Is A Warm Welcome	121
11	On The Doorstep, Under The Mat	131
12	Insider Trading	141
13	Home Alone	153
14	Bourbon And Water	160
15	Cloudy With A Chance Of Battle	167
16	It Takes A Thief In The Night	175
17	Battle Of Six Or Seven Armies	181
18	The Long Goodbyes	191
19	The Last Laugh	198

Chapter 1

AN UNEXPECTED BRUNCH

In a wholly below-ground apartment there lived a wobbit. His apartment was not as nasty, dirty, and wet as a hole, but it wasn't as fresh, bright and fun as a beach house. It was definitely at the "nasty" end of the home spectrum. Plants can cheer a place up, but the wobbit's apartment only had the mold in the walls and the mildew in the bathtub. It was a basement apartment, and that means fungus.

The wobbit was not very well-to-do, and his name was Bunkins. He worked as a barista at a local coffee bar, which was honest work, at least. Prior to that he was in banking.

The Bunkinses had lived in the village of Wobbiton, in the modest Bug End neighborhood, since time out of mind. The Bunkins in our story rented his basement apartment from Virginia, who also owned the beauty parlor in front of the building. He liked the location. There was a laundromat nearby, where he could wash and dry his little waistcoats and corduroy pants.

Bunkins kept to himself, avoiding block parties and yard sales. Talking with his wobbit neighbors always left him feeling inferior. The neighbors felt this was because Bunkins was truly inferior, even to other wobbits. Despite his solitary behavior, everyone knew all about Bunkins because of his ancestors. For generations, Bunkinses had been so stodgy and predictable that if you knew one of them, you knew them all. No one ever wanted to know more than one.

This is a story of how a Bunkins had an adventure, doing things that he found terrifying and saying things he normally kept to himself. In the end he still couldn't earn the neighbors' respect, but he gained a fortune and a magic ring that—but perhaps I'm getting ahead of myself.

The mother of our particular wobbit—what the hell is a wobbit? I suppose wobbits need some description, since they have become rare and shy of Big People With Good Jobs. They are short, really short, and this is accentuated by their poor posture. Wobbits are so short they regularly get beaten up by leprechauns. Wobbits are so short they are shorter than most children, even their own. Wobbits are so short some of them have legs that aren't long enough to touch the ground. You get the idea.

They have no beards, not even neck beards or patchy Van Dykes. There is little magic about them, except for the everyday sort that helps them disappear quietly if you ask them to help you move or take you to the airport. They wear no shoes, which makes it impossible for them to dine at non-wobbit restaurants. Their feet are hairy and large, although really they may just look large since wobbits overall are so short. Like the way horizontal stripes make you look fat.

As I was saying, the mother of this particular wobbit—Bulbo Bunkins, that is—was the fabulous Primadonna Dork. It was said that long ago one of her Dork ancestors must have taken a fairy husband, but this was based on several sad misunderstandings of the fairy lifestyle. The Dorks were regarded by most wobbits as "queer," and that's saying a lot. They were forever indulging odd interests, drifting aimlessly from comic book conventions to wargame tournaments to renaissance faires.

By some curious chance one morning long ago in the quiet of the world, when there was less noise and more disease spread by rats and raw sewage, and while Bulbo was standing at his door enjoying a large hazelnut latte and an even larger breakfast burrito —Pantsoff came by. Pantsoff! If you have heard a quarter of what I've heard about him, then I've heard 400% of what you've heard.

Not much of it is true, of course. The one really remarkable thing about Pantsoff was his brilliance in self-promotion. This is why, after his long absence, wobbits considered him legendary, like Paul Bunyan or Robert

Downey Jr. He carried a stick with a magical blue top, and wore immense black wing-tip boots. Around his neck he wrapped a scarf that was pure affectation.

He had a long, bushy moustache. If he didn't keep it trimmed it stuck out further than the brim of his shady-looking leather hat. Older wobbits who had seen Pantsoff years ago believed that it was actually nose hair run wild. This was because most elderly wobbits had to trim their nose hair constantly.

"Good morning!" said Bulbo, and he meant it. But Pantsoff just looked at him from over his bushy moustache.

"What do you mean?" he finally said. "What do you mean by 'good' and what do you mean by 'morning?'"

"Um, what?" said Bulbo.

"Enough small talk," said Pantsoff. "I'm here to make you the offer of a lifetime! I'm looking for someone to share a short, simple adventure that I'm arranging. So short and simple, in fact, that I thought of you immediately!"

I just met this guy, and already he's doing 'short' jokes, Bulbo thought. But he decided to be the bigger man, and so he remained polite.

"Here in Wobbiton we are a plain, dull folk," said Bulbo. "We have no use for adventures. They use up all your vacation days and interrupt your lawn care." He looked into the distance, as if he was totally involved in enjoying his latte. But the old man didn't move or say anything more.

"Good morning!" Bulbo said at last. "I don't buy Girl Scout cookies, so I'm certainly not going on any adventures that recruit door-to-door. You might try somewhere else, like Bug Heights or Bugland Park or West Bugville." He took a huge bite of burrito, and it squirted salsa on Pantsoff.

"What a lot of things you use *Good Morning* for!" said Pantsoff. "Too bad you can't use it to remove salsa stains. I just bought this wizard robe at Ye Olde Navie."

"Have we met?" said Bulbo. "I don't think I know your name."

"No—but I know yours, Mr. Bulbo Bunkins." This was not very impressive, since Bulbo was wearing his name tag from the coffee bar.

"And you know my name, though you don't remember that I belong to it. I am Pantsoff, and Pantsoff means me! That's right, me! Pantsoff! To think that I should live to be good-morninged by Primadonna Dork's son, as if I were selling adjustable rate mortgages door to door!"

"Pantsoff!" said Bulbo. "Not the wandering wizard that gave the Old Dork some magic ruby slippers that would take him home when he forgot where he lived? Not the fellow who used to tell such wonderful tales at parties, about the Man From Nantucket and the Young Wench From Peru? Not the Pantsoff who was responsible for so many frivolous lawsuits and Ponzi schemes? I beg your pardon, but I had no idea you were out of jail."

"I was never in jail!" said the wizard. "I made a deal with the D.A. Too bad my colleagues were all so obviously guilty. All the same, I am pleased to find you remember something about me. I may give you what you asked for."

"You'll give me your pardon?"

"No, I'll give you an immense black wing-tip to your little tuchas! You've been asking for it ever since you got salsa on me. Fortunately for you, though, I need your butt intact for the adventure you're going on."

"Sorry! I don't want any adventures, thank you. Good morning!" But Pantsoff still wouldn't move. Bulbo reconsidered his rudeness, just in case any of the old stories about Pantsoff were true. He added a polite, if insincere, postscript.

"Please stop by for brunch tomorrow, it's my day off. Yes, brunch tomorrow, that's the ticket!" And with that the wobbit turned and scuttled, as only wobbits and hermit crabs can, back into his hole, shutting the round screen door as quickly as he dared.

"What was I thinking?" he asked himself as he went to the kitchenette. He thought a drink might steady his nerves. There was a crusty bottle of blackberry brandy that had been around too long. Dreadful or not, it would do.

Pantsoff in the meantime was lurking outside. After a while he stepped up and stenciled a queer sign, queer even to Dorkish eyes, on the wobbit's aluminum (or al-u-minium, as the wobbits called it) screen door. Then he slunk away, as

8

Bulbo finished his second cocktail. Bulbo was so shaken he took a sick day.

The next morning Bulbo had forgotten all about Pantsoff and the brunch invitation. He did not remember appointments very well, unless he wrote them in his Elfkin Planner, like this: *Unemployment check-in call today.* The day before he had been too busy with his expired bottle of blackberry brandy to document his invitation to Pantsoff, bogus though it was.

Just before eleven there came a knock at the screen door, amplified and made rattly by its ricketyness, and then he remembered! He quickly started some eggs, cut a few melon wedges and looked for champagne to make mimosas. He decided to serve the unpleasant blackberry brandy instead, and ran for the door.

"Fashionably early, Pantsoff!" he said, and then he saw it was not Pantsoff at all. It was a dwarf with a long, black jazz beard tucked into a cordovan belt. The dwarf entered abruptly and said "Crawlin of SmithiBank. My card." He presented a business card that said he was on the board of directors at "SmithiBank: *The Bank for metalsmiths, miners and engineers. Serving the Dwarf and Kobold community since the Second Age.*"

"Um, hi. I'm Bulbo Bunkins. Look, I'm expecting an old friend from out of town, so you'll have to leave. You understand. Hey, I used to work for SmithiBank, too! I was a teller at the Wobbiton branch."

"Yes, isn't it a small world? No offense. Do I smell frittata?"

Bulbo ignored the "small world" insult. He was trying to come up with a response more to the point than his original "you'll have to leave" when there was another rattly knock at the screen door.

"I'm actually relieved you're here, Pantsoff," Bulbo said at the door, but it still wasn't Pantsoff. Instead, it was another dwarf, this one very old, with white mutton chop sideburns. He pushed past Bulbo.

"Fallin, board member at SmithiBank. My card," he said. "I see they have begun to arrive already."

"What is going on here?" Bulbo wondered. "What do these dwarves want? SmithiBank is washed up, but these former big-shots probably know some other bankers that are still successful. Should I let them stay and look at it as a networking opportunity? If I could get back into banking, I'd at least have health insurance again." While unemployed, Bulbo had been able to keep his SmithiBank insurance under the B.A.S.I.L.I.S.K. program, but his payments had been, in a word, monstrous.

"I'll let them stay for some coffee," decided Bulbo, but he was interrupted by Fallin.

"I'll have a vodka screwdriver and an egg white omelet."

There was more rapping at the door. As you might expect at this point, it wasn't Pantsoff, but more dwarves, with more SmithiBank board member business cards. They had odd facial hair, and weird names. Wheeli and Deali, in fact.

"Get us some Krispy Kremes," they said.

"In a minute," said Bulbo. "Is this a reunion for you guys? Wouldn't a hotel have been better? There's a Best Uttermost-Western just down the road, and they've got a lounge. You look like big drinkers."

"Where's the carving station for the ham?" Crawlin asked. "I want mine sliced off the bone," he said.

"I'll give you a bone," said Bulbo, when there was another knock. More dwarves, funny names, cards, beards, and demands for food. It went on like this for some time, but you'd probably be just as happy if I gave you all their names at once and kept the dialogue to a minimum, so here they are: Rori, Tori, and Gori, as well as Loin and Groin, Beefi and Bufu, and Fatso followed them.

Right behind Fatso came the pushiest and most presumptive of them all. It was, in fact, none other than the Chairman Of The Board at SmithiBank, the great Borin Oakmanfield. But Fatso had got his hand caught in Bulbo's shoddy screen door, and Borin stumbled over him. The resulting pile-up of dwarves in Bulbo's foyer would have been funny if only it were happening in someone else's apartment. Pantsoff, who arrived last, definitely considered it funny.

"Bulbo, my lad, these dwarves are more fun than the Elf Pride Parade," he said. He then gleefully poked at them with his stick, which he called either a wand or a staff, depending on his mood. "Gads, I'm parched. What's that? A blackberry brandy cooler? No thank you! Single-malt scotch for me. A Glenlivet."

"And for me" said Borin.

"Make mine Glenfiddich," said Beefi.

"Glennclose for me" said Bufu.

"Glengaryglenross for me," said Fatso, "with a splash of low-carb water, if you have any."

"Whip up some scones, there's a good fellow!" Pantsoff called after him. "And just bring out the sliders and spring rolls!"

"If I snuck out the back door, how long would I have to stay away before they all left?" thought Mr. Bunkins. He rarely entertained, so soon every dish, glass, thermal travel mug, vase and commemorative plate was in use. He was feeling positively flummoxed.

"Jeez Louise!" he said aloud. "Would it kill them to give me some help?" Lo and behold—there stood Borin Oakmanfield.

"I'd give you some help," Borin said, "but my doctor says it would kill me. I have a rare condition. But perhaps some of my vice presidents could be incentivized to help."

"Would our bonuses be based on performance?" Crawlin asked.

"Of course, and we're all doing excellent work, as usual. If it weren't for the current financial crisis, I would simply declare 'Mission Accomplished' and we could all consider this adventure a success. But since we dwarves have fallen on hard times we can no longer reward ourselves as we once did. So hop to it. And let's have a song, while you're at it."

So the dwarves started singing, some as they cleaned up, and some as they continued to eat and drink, which was not a pretty sight. Wobbits have a high tolerance for poor table manners, but the sight of a dozen dwarves working and

11

singing with their mouths and beards full was unforgettable.
They kept this up while washing and putting away the "clean"
dishes. Bulbo's kitchenette soon looked like a crime scene at
a juice bar. The good news was that the dwarves had lovely
singing voices, and the tune was familiar:

Bulbo Bunkins has a hole
Ee-I, Ee-I, Oh!
And in his hole he had some plates
Ee, Heigh-Ho, Heigh-Ho!
With a chipped glass here and a bent fork there
Spill the wine, spill the beer, everywhere we spill, spill
That's what Bulbo Bunkins hates
Ee, Heigh-Ho, Heigh-Ho!

Scrub the silver with your beard
Ee, Heigh-Ho, Heigh-Ho!
Lick the plates until they're clean
Ee, Heigh-Ho, Heigh-Ho!
With a beard-scrubbed spoon and a plate licked clean
Here a beard, there a lick, Bulbo's getting sick, sick
That's what Bulbo Bunkins hates
Ee, Heigh-Ho, Heigh-Ho!

Spit and polish for the kettle,
Ee, Heigh-Ho, Heigh-Ho!
Spit and polish all the metal
Ee, Heigh-Ho, Heigh-Ho!
With a polish here and a spit spit there
Here a spit, there a spit, everywhere we spit, spit
That's what Bulbo Bunkins hates
Ee, Heigh-Ho, Heigh-Ho!

The only thing Bulbo found more nauseating than the
dwarf-cleaning of his kitchenette was the smell of their pipe-
smoke throughout his apartment. Borin had his feet on
Bulbo's coffee table, blowing smoke rings. Bulbo tried to
find a small area of "fresh" air, which was not easy, given a
large group of dwarves in a small space. Wherever he went,
Borin's smoke-rings followed him.

The smell was dizzying. It was terrible tobacco. If you were to make onion dip for a picnic, and then put the bowl in a sinkful of water, then turn off the air conditioning, and then return from the picnic two days later, the smell that greeted you would be similar to the smell that surrounded Bulbo. Pantsoff was smoking, too. His smoke was all in a cloud around his head, and in the dim light it made him look strange and nauseous.

"Now for some real music!" said Borin. "Bring out the instruments!"

"Oh no" thought Bulbo. Sure enough, Wheeli and Deali brought out kazoos. Rori, Tori and Gori found some nose flutes. Fatso started warming up on mandolin. Beefi and Bufu got their spoons. Fallin and Crawlin found tambourines with long ribbons. Borin was handed a massive, iron-bound banjo. Bulbo would never have guessed that an instrument with only five strings would take so long to tune, but perhaps Borin had been slowed down by drinking so much of Bulbo's scotch.

All at once, like a hangover-induced "urgency," the dwarves began. As they played, Bulbo listened and forgot about the broken dishes and everything else as darkness filled the room.

Borin began singing. Bulbo was swept away into dark lands under strange moons, to the waters of the western coast. He had never heard these dwarven words, but the tune sounded familiar. It reminded him of a song he knew, from the far Hills Of Beverly:

> Come and listen to the story 'bout a group of dwarves
> Opened up a bank in the days of ancient yore
> Past the Moisty Mountains standing tall and cold
> Our boardrooms were dark and our bank guards were old
> (Business, that is. Loans made. Dwarven tea.)
>
> Well the first thing you know we made a lot of loans
> To lake folks, for their shops and farms and homes
> Said: "The Only Mountain is the place you want to be"
> So we built our corporate home there for everyone to see
> (Hubris, that is. Dragon came. Burned the town.)
>
> Well the next thing you know the loans were not repaid

13

We all ran away, although we're very brave
Said "No foreclosures since Lake City is burned down
With so many of our borrowers eaten or drowned"
(Bankrupt, that is. No loan income. No fee income.)

Well now we all have said goodbye
        to home and dwarven kin
We swore we'd kill the dragon
        and rebuild our bank again
Our stock will soar, champagne we'll pour at this locality
Come have a heaping helping of our hospitality
Dwarf, that is
Sit a spell
Take your boots off
Ye all come back now, aye!

As they sang, Bulbo felt the love of easy money, a fierce and jealous love. He felt the dwarven desire for a classic Get Ye Riche Quick Scheme. Something Dorkish woke up inside him, desiring wealth to expand his collection of Rootball memorabilia.

Rootball is a purely wobbit sport which Bulbo had long enjoyed, but only as a spectator. It involved two groups of large wobbits, some of them towering almost four feet tall, chasing each other in an open field, trying to capture a large potato (or rutabaga) and throwing it back and forth. Team jerkins were easy to find, but expensive. Game balls were almost impossible to come by for any amount, since they were usually consumed by the players.

Bulbo thought about his future collection, and then got up to review his current one and plan his necessary purchases. He couldn't wait to spend his share from the dwarf job, even though he had not yet been invited to join.

"Where are you going?" said Borin. Bulbo knew then that Borin had guessed at his secret greed. Bulbo comforted himself with the thought *"It takes one to know one,"* as old *Primadonna Dork used to say.*

"I'm thirsty," said Bulbo. "Anyone else want a light beer?"

"We want dark beer," said all the dwarves. "Dark beer for dark business."

14

"Let me go out for some" said Bulbo, as he put his foot in a bucket. He clanked about for a bit until he stepped on a rake by the door. It hit him in the eye and knocked him against a folding table where the dwarves had put their instruments from the last musical number. It collapsed loudly.

"Hush!" said Pantsoff. "Let the big shot speak!" And this is how Borin began.

"Pantsoff, dwarves, and Mr. Bunkins! We are met together in the home of our friend and fellow conspirator; a most excellent and audacious wobbit—may the hair in his ears never fall out! All praise his free bar!" He paused, awaiting a polite reply from the wobbit, but Bulbo was busy looking for a way out with his uninjured eye. Given Borin's famous policy at SmithiBank of "if you're not caught, it's not a crime," being called his "fellow conspirator" was deeply upsetting.

"Harumph! As we plan our journey I would be remiss in my duties as Chief Executive Officer of the New Improved Smithi Financial Solutions if I failed to point out the peril of our undertaking. It is financially sound, but physically speculative in nature. In fact, lethally so. Some of us may never return. I will be surprised and somewhat disappointed if at least three of us are not killed. As you look at page 41 of the prospectus, you will see a partial list of the bloody mayhem that awaits us." He passed out some documents.

"Before each of you signs the Personal Liability Waiver, I will read item 26.4 aloud: 'This journey is not bonded or insured. You could lose body parts or your entire life. Your projected survivability is based on past performance, which does not guarantee a future return from the journey. Your results may vary.' Skip ahead to page 78 and—"

This was Borin's style. The dwarves and Pantsoff were starting to doze. Borin would have gone on until they all were fast asleep, himself included, but Bulbo couldn't bear it any longer.

At the words *may never return* he felt a shriek coming on, as all Dorks do from time to time. They tend to be highly emotional, which they sometimes express in "inappropriate" ways: crying at the store, fighting with waitresses, resisting arrest, that sort of thing. So, as many of his forefathers did in days of yore, Bulbo shrieked like a little girl.

Startled, the dwarves all sprang up at the sudden, piercing noise. Pantsoff reflexively cast a spell to defend himself. There was the sound of thunder, the blue tip at the end of his staff flashed magically, and then, nothing. The spell was supposed to shrink its victim to half the size of a man, but since the target was the terrified Bulbo, nothing else happened.

"Sorry about that," said Pantsoff, but Bulbo could only call out "Struck by irony! Struck by irony!" over and over again from a fetal position on the floor. Irony always had a profound effect on Bulbo.

"Excitable little fellow," said Pantsoff. "Gets funny queer fits as all Dorks do, but he's as fierce as a dragon in a pinch."

Borin turned to pinch Bulbo, just to see if Pantsoff was telling the truth, but Bulbo had crawled away to sulk. If you've ever seen a dragon being pinched, you will realize this was a poetical exaggeration applied to any wobbit. It would be an exaggeration even if applied to Old Dork's great-grand-uncle Bullshitter, who was so huge (for a wobbit) that he could ride a big-boy roller coaster. He became famous for negotiating peace with the goblins by challenging their King Golfouting to a long morning walk, followed by an afternoon of drinking, giving the king a splitting headache the next day. This resulted in a swiftly negotiated peace and the invention of Golf at the same moment.

Bulbo had none of his great-grand-uncle's courage, but all of his drinking capacity. While sulking, he looked for any remaining scotch. Finding a bottle of Glenorglenda that had escaped the dwarves, he took a long swig from it. He was attempting to black out the entire experience. But he couldn't help eavesdropping on the dwarves.

He heard Groin speaking. "Humph! Will he do, do you think? That shriek would have been embarrassing at a bachelorette party. How is he going to manage dragon hunting? I get my beard highlighted by two guys named Bob and Matt, and either one of them is fiercer than shorty over there."

Then Mr. Bunkins spoke up. His giddy Dork side, and the scotch, had overcome his normal Bunkins stodginess.

"Okay, Mr. Highlighted Beard," he said. "I was a teller when I worked for you SmithiBank guys at your Wobbiton branch. I never met any of you, but I didn't like you. No one at our branch liked you, and I still don't. And you have come to the wrong hole. There's no sign on my door but I really need a job, so make me an offer. I'm up for it. I had a great-great-grand-uncle once, Bullshitter Dork, and—"

"Yes, yes, and he invented Golf, but that was long ago," said Groin. "I was talking about you, half-pint. And there is a mark on the door. *Burglar with demonstrated sneaking skills seeks immediate position with opportunity for personal development.* That's how it's usually read. You may say *Consultant* instead of *Burglar* if you like. Most of them do. We heard about you from Pantsoff, when he invited us to this meet-and-greet."

"You invited them?" Bulbo howled. "These pigs drink me out of hole and home and—"

"Bulbo, my lad, I'll pay you back of course," Pantsoff said. "But who cares? Don't you want to get rich? And there is a sign on your door which I put there, excellent work, too. You'll never get that paint off! But let's not quibble, Groin. Bulbo is your burglar and I'm sure he'll be able to learn on the job. If you disagree, I'll resign and Borin may begin his search for a new project manager. Any other concerns?" Pantsoff waited but Bulbo, Groin and Borin remained silent.

"Great. We ought to take a look at the map I've brought. It was made by Floor, your grandfather, Borin." Borin shot him a look that said, *Yes, I know he's my grandfather.* "On one side is a connect-the-dots and a word-search, and on the other is a map of the mountain. It shows One SmithiBank Plaza, Lake City, the dragon, and we're here, where it says 'You are here.' The plan is this: Bulbo is going to sneak in through a service entrance using this key, and then you just improvise the rest. Believe me, getting past that locked door is your biggest challenge. Killing the dragon should be relatively easy, perhaps best left to Bulbo. He'll figure it out when the time comes. What questions to you have?"

"What's this about a dragon?" asked Bulbo.

"Weren't you paying attention to the lyrics during the banjo and mandolin number? The map? The prospectus?" said Borin. "Really, Pantsoff, is this guy the best you could do? Fine, we'll sing our theme song again."

The dwarves sang it again. "I'm still not getting it," said Bulbo. "Could you do an interpretive dance, instead? Or maybe just tell me?"

"Oh very well," said Borin. "My grandfather, Floor, built SmithiBank up from nothing, from a little building & loan into a banking monolith. Depositors from far and wide brought us their gold and jewels. Borrowers came to us for mortgages. Through outsourcing, automation and lots of hidden fees we made SmithiBank huge and very profitable. But mortgages became the source of our greatest wealth, and our downfall. Back in those days, being in the mortgage business was like having a license to print money, which Floor also had, for a time. He guaranteed his stockholders unlimited prosperity forever, but perhaps he was being unrealistic. In any event, SmithiBank soon became the largest issuer of mortgages in all of Little Earth, especially near the Only Mountain, in Lake City.

"As happens from time to time, a dragon showed up and adjusted the market, ruining everything. His name was Smog, and he moved into Lake City. All the wise men and analysts said this would cause a huge loss of equity, and then Lake City property quickly devalued. Investor confidence failed and depositors, especially the gremlins and brownies, would have withdrawn all their gold and jewels if Smug wasn't sitting on them.

"We tried to sell some of the loans to recover. We tried to recapitalize. Nothing worked, and all that's left of our bank is a portfolio of near-worthless loans, a pile of treasure, and a corporate office plaza occupied by a dragon. My grandfather and I and the few board members you see here were the only employees to escape Smug. When the attack on the mountain began, my board and I were away entertaining clients on a Lake City booze cruise, and Floor bravely ducked out the service entrance that Pantsoff mentioned. But the key was thought to be lost when my grandfather suddenly left to hike the Moisty Mountain Trail. Pantsoff, just how did you get hold of it?"

"I didn't 'get hold of it,' I was given it" said the wizard. "Your grand father was killed, you remember, in the Moisty Mountains, by Agog the Goblin King."

"Yes, I do remember that," Borin said. "Floor was my grandfather, after all."

"Indeed," Pantsoff continued. "We had run into each other at the Goblin King's Moisty Mountain summer home. It turns out we were both there to, um, visit Agog's wife, the Goblin Queen. But the Goblin King arrived unexpectedly and we thought it best to leave. I quickly took the lead, to clear a path for my friend. He was lagging behind so I went back to help. He had needlessly weighed himself down with valuables, so I took the key and some of his other heavy personal items, like the map. He didn't make it out, but I did my best, so on the whole I ought to be praised and thanked!"

"Let me get this straight," said Bulbo. "Pantsoff, even though you're the brains of this outfit, you want me, a consultant and former teller, to figure out how to get rid of a dragon?"

"That's it exactly, my boy! You've cut right to the heart of the matter. You're even more perfect for this project than I thought! Everyone, look how he's thinking outside the strong-box!"

Realizing that this was the best job offer he'd had in a long time, Bulbo decided to sleep on it. Instead of leaving, the few dwarves that hadn't passed out yet went to sleep where they were. Bulbo's fanciful Dorkish side was being chased away by his boring Bunkins-ness. He was hoping that he would wake up tomorrow to discover that this was all a dream. A smelly, insulting dream.

As he folded out his Murphy bed from the wall, he could hear Borin still humming to himself. Oddly, the humming had lyrics:

Our stock will soar, champagne we'll pour at this locality

Come have a heaping helping of our hospitality
Dwarf, that is
Sit a spell
Take your boots off
Ye all come back now, aye!

Bulbo went to sleep with the song in his ear. The song, and also one of Fatso's fingers. It was really crowded in Bulbo's apartment. He would soon discover, to his disappointment, that the dwarves' visit wasn't a dream.

Chapter 2

MUTTON ROAST, $2.95 LB.

Up jumped Bulbo, pulling on his corduroy pants. The dwarves were gone, but they had re-dirtied every dish in the kitchenette, in some cases with actual dirt. They hadn't attempted to clean up, but based on the unhygienic habits Bulbo had seen the night before, he was happy to have a chance to wash his dishes personally. Using soap and water this time. *Just to be on the safe side,* he thought. He felt elated that the dwarves and Pantsoff had gone on without him. At the same time, he could not help feeling disappointed. He fought that feeling.

"Don't be an idiot, Bulbo Bunkins!" he said to himself. "Thinking of dragons and equity! Ridiculous!" He found a bag of pretzels he'd hidden and a light beer, the only beverage the dwarves wouldn't drink. This made a nice little breakfast as he reassured himself. Better job offers would come along, full-time ones with benefits. Not consulting. Not killing dragons. Not for SmithiBank. Not with Pantsoff.

Bulbo was happily opening his second beer when in walked Pantsoff.

"My dear fellow," he said. "Whenever are you going to come? The dwarves left you a message, because they could not wait."

"Oh no!" said Bulbo.

"Great elephants!" said Pantsoff. "How could you miss it? It's stuck to your bathroom mirror!"

In fairness to Bulbo, thirteen dwarves had just spent the night, so there were lots of things stuck to the bathroom mirror. Gingerly, Bulbo removed and read the note:

21

"Re: Contractor Employment

Mr. Bunkins-
      Welcome to the New, Improved SmithiBank
(Smithi Financial Solutions)! Effective immediately,
you are hired to provide personal services to
SmithiBank and its board members, up to and
including your killing of the dragon known as Smog.
You will be paid a one-fourteenth share of the net
proceeds of said killing within 90 days of its
satisfactory completion.
      It is mission-critical that you meet us at the
Ass-Dragon Inn of West Bugville at 11:00.

Borin Oakmanfield, CEO
New, Improved Smithi Financial Solutions"

"That leaves you just ten minutes. You will have to
run," said Pantsoff.
      "But—" said Bulbo.
      "No time for that! Just write a quick note to your
landlady asking her to sublet your apartment while you're
gone. I'll give it to her, and your key, too. Off you go!"
      To the end of his days, Bulbo never forgave Pantsoff
for bouncing him out of his own hole without a chance to stop
delivery of his Wobbiton Shopper. Wincing at the pain from
his lower back, he ran past the Best Uttermost Western Motel,
past the Ye Olde Navie, past the Gristle Mill, and then he ran
out of breath. He walked the rest of the way.
      Very puffed he was, like a cheap cigar, when he saw a
sign depicting a donkey and a reptile in an unwholesome
embrace. He had arrived at the Ass-Dragon Inn. He realized
that he had left his wallet back in his hole.
      Just then, the rest of the New, Improved SmithiBank
arrived outside, each dwarf on a small pony. The assembly
looked like a disreputable petting zoo. They were loaded with
briefcases, golf bags, brochures and paraphernalia. Bulbo's
Dorkish nature was immediately drawn to the paraphernalia.

"Off we go!" called Borin. "I'm not paying you to stand around!"

"What kind of adventure is this?" said Bulbo. "Why didn't you tell me we were leaving so soon? You could have included that in one of your songs! I don't even have my wallet!"

"Good," said Crawlin. "Fewer documents to destroy if we have to bury you in a shallow grave. Anyway, you can just sign for any of your expenses on the way and we'll deduct it from your share at the end. Assuming you survive. We'll keep track of everything, like your food and your pony rental. You might want to buy one of our extra cloaks, as well."

That's how they all came to start, with Bulbo in a too-large second-hand travel-cloak purchased at a hotel lobby boutique price. His only comfort was that he couldn't be mistaken for a dwarf, as he had no beard and he wasn't spitting.

They had not been riding very long when up came Pantsoff on a white horse. "Don't I look splendid?" he said. Bulbo tried to stop and talk with him, but he refused.

"No time, Bulbo," he said. "I didn't actually get the approval of Buttercup's owner before I borrowed her. We need to put a few furlongs between him and me as soon as possible." Pantsoff galloped on ahead.

When they next saw Pantsoff, the country had already started to change. They came to lands where people (meaning wobbits) refused to belch politely after every meal: the taverns were much quieter and they weren't as "stuffy." They used strange words, like "catsup" instead of ketchup, and they wrote their "S"s like "F"s. They sang songs that Bulbo had never heard before, some of them by Hootie And The Blowfish. What started out as delightful May weather soon became crappy May weather, rainy and cold. It was long past cocktail time.

"The only thing worse for my back than the cold and damp is riding this wretched pony," grumbled Bulbo.

"You think *your* back hurts?" neighed the pony. Since Bulbo wasn't an elf, the insult went over his head. As did many things.

23

"Bother consulting and everything to do with it!" said Bulbo. I wish I was back in my nice hole mixing up a Manhattan!" It was not the last time he wished that!

Bulbo wished for cocktails and his La-Z-Boy so often that the dwarves would have been irritated if they still noticed him. They were hardly aware of him at all any more. Like when a friend doesn't notice that their house smells like their dog. In fact, there were a lot of smells the dwarves didn't notice.

They did notice that Pantsoff was gone. Despite his role as the adventure's Project Manager, Pantsoff had not yet done anything to actually help, other than his controversial addition of Bulbo to the group. Mostly, he talked, saying things like "Don't I look splendid on my white horse?" and "Are you going to finish that sandwich, Bulbo?" He laughed a lot, too, especially if he finished eating one of Bulbo's meals before Bulbo was done with it. If Bulbo hadn't been secretly snacking during the entire adventure, he would have starved.

"Pantsoff must have found a wedding reception to crash," grumbled Tori and Rori. They shared Bulbo's views about Pantsoff being a skilled shyster and little else.

The rain started to let up. The wind broke up the grey clouds, and a wandering moon appeared above the hills between the flying rags. Then the company stopped. "Quit throwing rags, you guys!" said Borin. "We need to find a dry patch to sleep on."

They moved to a clump of trees that was drier underneath, but the wind shook the rain off the leaves, and the drip, drip was most annoying to Bulbo. It was like camping beneath a great, runny nose. Dwarves' noses run as a matter of course, so they didn't mind.

It was impossible for them to start a fire. Normally, dwarves can make a fire with as little as a single subpoenaed document, but not that night. Soon, Loin and Groin put away their massive, iron-bound butane lighters, glumly blaming each other for their failure.

Borin was preparing to silence them with a "Harumph" when Fallin, their lookout dwarf, said "There's a light over there! Or maybe it's a sasquatch. No, no, it's a light!" After some argument, the dwarves all agreed that it was not a sasquatch or even a yeti, but definitely a light. They further agreed that they should investigate, hoping for a hot meal and dry clothes. They argued about whether undertaking the investigation would be "dangerous" or "very dangerous." But they did not argue about who would undertake it.

"Bulbo!" they acclaimed as one. They picked up their consultant and crept closer to the light, quietly as they could in their hobnail boots and bronze boxer shorts.

"Now it is the consultant's turn," said Borin. "You must go on and find out if it's safe. If we hear you being killed, or if you don't return because you were killed silently, we'll look for another campsite. Now, Bulbo, just sneak off and—"

"You mean 'scuttle off,' don't you?" Fallin suggested.

"Yes, of course. Scuttle off, Bulbo, like the little wobbit you are, and come back as soon as you can, if you can. If you can't, we'll do our best without you. The money you owe us for the food, pony and coat will be billed to your estate, and we'll split the treasure thirteen ways instead of fourteen."

Off Bulbo had to go, since his job description required it. Scuttle he did, but quietly, absolutely quietly, as only wobbits can. They take pride in being able to silently leave a bar if there's a tab to be paid, or to secretly enter one if there's a cover charge. Bulbo sniffed frequently at what he called "all the dwarvish racket," and unlike the dwarves, his frequent sniffing had nothing to do with a head cold or an athelas allergy. So, naturally, he got right up to the fire without disturbing anyone. And this is what he saw.

Three very large persons sitting around a very large fire of lincoln logs. They were toasting mutton on long and very large spits of wood. *Spit-roasting. Who does that remind me of?* Bulbo thought. They were licking the gravy off their fingers, and in some cases, off each other's fingers. *Like I said before.* They were drinking what smelled like, from their belches, corn whiskey out of jugs. *Again.* Were it not for their lack of beards and their size, which was very large, Bulbo would have assumed them to be dwarf-kin of Borin's, and possibly escaped SmithiBank board members. But they did not have dwarf haircuts. The first one had a crew cut, the second was bald on top with long, frizzy hair over the ears, and the third looked like his hair had been cut using a bowl. A very large bowl. They were trolls. Obviously trolls. Bulbo could tell by their language, which was not especially large, but very unusual.

"There ain't enough mutton here to feed a mouse," said one of the trolls. "And that's all there is! Mutton, mutton, who wants more mutton? Nyuk nyuk nyuk!"

"I'm dying, I tell ya, dying," said another. "What's the big idea! Bringing us to the middle of nowhere! Starving us on nothing but lousy mutton, and now the hooch is running low. What gives, Joe?" He jogged the elbow of Joe, who was taking a pull at his jug.

Joe choked. "Dying, are ya? I'll show you 'dying!'" He grabbed Harry's nose and pulled his head toward the fire until his frizzy hair started to smoke on one side.

"Ow ow ow ow ow ow ow ow!" Harry moaned.

"This is the thanks I get," Joe continued. "Looking after you two lame brains. You can't expect people to stop here just to be eaten by you and Shirley. Come here, you numbskulls." When Harry and Shirley leaned in, Joe slapped both of them with one sweeping motion of his hand. The two smacks were much louder than Bulbo expected.

Yes, I am afraid trolls really do act like that, even those that wear white bib overalls, as these did. Even though one was a guy named Shirley. After hearing all this, Bulbo should have done something at once. Either he should have gone back quietly and told his employers that there were three trolls interested in submitting resumes for the SmithiBank Collections Department, or he should have done a quick bit of consulting. A really first-class and legendary consultant would have consulted the trolls' pockets until they were empty. Another, perhaps being hired as an independent contractor, would have stuck a dagger into each of the trolls before they noticed it. Then the night could have been spent cheerily, using the three very large corpses as picnic benches or cots.

Bulbo knew it. He had read enough self-help books to know a good many things about pick pocketing and backstabbing. Like most Dorks, though, he didn't realize the difference between reading about something and being able to do it. He assumed that reading "Ten Steps Towards Ye Olde Tighter Abs" was all it took to have tighter abs, despite the wealth of evidence to the contrary. This led Bulbo to believe that he might finally be able to impress Borin & Company. If things went well enough, they might issue him his own sleeping bag, and he wouldn't have to cuddle up with Fatso anymore. Bulbo plucked up his courage, crept very close, and put his sweaty little hand in Shirley's pocket.

"Ha!" thought he, warming to his new work, "I've got it!"

And get it he did. Trolls' pockets are mischief, and have more in them than skulls and receipts from deductible expenses. This pocket was no exception.

"EEE OOO OWW EEE!" Bulbo shrieked as he pulled out his hand with a mousetrap clamped on it.

"Joe! Harry! Fellas, come here. Lookit what I caught!" said the troll, grabbing the wobbit. He held Bulbo up in front of his face, barking and growling at him.

"Take it easy, champ. Say, what's that thing you've caught? What are you?" asked Harry.

"I'm Bulbo Bunkins, a consultant," said poor Bulbo, as he wondered how he would get the cleaning deposit back on the pants he'd rented from Borin.

"A consultant? What does a consultant do?" said Harry.

"Um, nothing. I mean, nobody knows!" squeaked Bulbo.

"Oh, a wise guy, eh?" said Joe. "Too bad you're so small. You're hardly worth cooking."

"Maybe there's more like him, and we could bake them into a Consultant Pie," said Harry. "If there's enough we could have a pie-fight!"

"You're starving, but you want to have a pie-fight!" Joe held up a hand with the fingers spread. "Pick two," he said.

Harry picked Joe's index and ring fingers, and Joe poked him in the eyes with them.

Why should that make a "doink" sound? Bulbo wondered, until he was interrupted.

"Well, stranger? Are there more of you?" Joe demanded.

"Oh yes, lots," said Bulbo without thinking. "If you spare me, I'll call them over," he said immediately afterwards.

"Spare you?" said Joe. "Why should we spare you? You're a traitor, ratting out the rest of your gang."

"Not really. I'm not part of their gang. You see, I'm a contractor, hired for this one adventure to work for them. They're all SmithiBank board members, and..."

"SmithiBank!" yelled Shirley, who suddenly head-butted Harry, and then fell to the ground. He started spinning like a coffee-grinder, howling "Woo woo woowoowoowoo!"

"Listen, kid," Joe said to Bulbo confidentially, "SmithiBank wouldn't give us a loan to expand our wallpaper-hanging business. Whenever Shirley hears the word 'SmithiBank' he goes nuts!

"Because of them, our business failed, and we're reduced to eating strangers we meet on the road." Shirley's fit died off as he was strangling Harry. "Just don't say the word," Joe lowered his voice, "'SmithiBank.'"

"Yes, fair enough," said Bulbo, eager to get back to his point. "So like I was saying, spare me and I'll lure all those lousy bankers over here. If you want, I'll even help you kill them and cook them!"

"Say, Jasper, you're all right," said Harry, and then they all shook hands as Shirley again laughed a strange "Nyuk nyuk nyuk." Bulbo decided against pointing out that his name was not "Jasper."

The hand shaking and laughing stopped when Fallin stepped into the light. The dwarves suspected that Bulbo was "up to something" and sent Fallin to follow up on his progress. He was even prepared to provide Bulbo with some coaching. But there was to be no coaching or even any feedback, because Fallin was soon hit on the head with a huge wooden mallet. As Bulbo wondered at the unusual "bonk" sound, Shirley put a sack over Fallin's head.

"There's more to come yet," said Bulbo quietly to Joe. "Do you have twelve more of those sacks?"

"Good thinking, pal!" said Joe. "Grab those bags, you mugs! Now spread out!"

And so they did. They had plenty of sacks nearby that they used when grocery shopping, to avoid the need for disposable bags. With these sacks in their hands, they waited in the shadows as each dwarf came up one at a time, like the bad guys in a Bruce Lee movie. Soon Crawlin lay by Fallin, Wheeli and Deali together, and Rori and Tori and Gori all in a heap, and Loin and Groin and Beefi and Bufu and Fatso piled uncomfortably near the fire.

Borin came last. He had sent every single one of his company, most of whom were also his relatives, into grave danger ahead of him. He called this "risk management."

He didn't need to see whiskey jugs, grilled meat, and twelve pair of cordovan hobnail boots sticking out of sacks to tell him things were not right. "What is this? An off-site team-building seminar? Well, there's no time! We're busy and important dwarves! I want to speak with the facilitator of this event immediately!"

"Borin!" said Bulbo from a hiding place. "Come closer! It's time for your keynote address!"

"Oh, well, of course," said Borin, and this is how he began. "Mr. Bunkins, dwarves, and trolls. We are met together in the—Trolls!" he yelled in surprise.

"We're trolls, and we're victims of circumstance!" said Shirley. "With the poor economy and all, we have to eat you and your pals! Nyuk nyuk nyuk!" He and the other trolls slowly approached from all sides, step by step, inch by inch.

"How dare you!" said Borin. "Stop right there. I'm Borin Oakmanfield, CEO of the New, Improved SmithiBank, and—"

"SmithiBank! Woo woo woowoowoowoo!" howled Shirley. He grabbed Borin with one hand and Harry with the other, and clunked their heads together. Then Shirley fell over and started spinning. Joe put Borin in a sack, and revived Harry by pinching his nose with a pliers. *It sounds like someone eating a carrot* Bulbo thought. When Shirley's fit wore off, all three trolls started arguing about how to cook the dwarves.

As trolls go, these three had very sophisticated tastes. One wanted to brine, batter-dip and deep fry them. Another wanted to fillet them and serve them in hand rolls of rice and seaweed. The third wanted to chop them into a soup with seasonal vegetables. Bulbo was hoping he would be completely forgotten.

It was just then that Pantsoff came back. But no one saw him or heard him, which was not normally Pantsoff's style. The trolls had just decided to slice Borin & Company thin and make them into dwarf jerky. It was Harry's favorite, and after a lot of argument they had all agreed to it.

"What's the big idea? It'll take forever to cut and dry all that dwarf-meat!" said a voice. Joe thought it was Harry's.

"Pipe down, chucklehead. We all agreed," said Joe.

"Pipe down yourself," said Harry. "I didn't say nothing."

"Oh, breaking ranks, eh? Why, I oughta—" said Joe as he reached towards Harry's ear with a serrated knife. He was interrupted by a voice that sounded like Shirley's.

"Joe! Harry! Cheese! Let's grill them on focaccia bread with artisan cheese. I want panini!"

"Quiet, you," said Joe.

"Who, me?" said Shirley as he reached for some whiskey. "You're hearing things. I ain't said a word. Now gimme that jug!"

"Not a word? Not even the word—SmithiBank?" The voice seemed to come from Joe.

"SmithiBank! Woo woo woowoowoowoo!" said Shirley. He then hit Joe and Harry each with the jug, knocking them cold. He looked around for someone else to attack, but found no one. He shrugged, laughed a final "Nyuk nyuk nyuk" to himself, and smashed the jug over his own head, falling on top of Joe and Harry in a very large pile.

"Take that! Serves you all right!" said a voice that sounded like Harry's. But it wasn't.

"Ta-daaah!" said Pantsoff, as he stepped from behind a tree, and he climbed atop the very large pile of trolls to take an unsteady bow. The dwarves did not applaud, because they were still in sacks. Bulbo didn't either, since he was quickly trying to confirm that the trolls were indeed out before he switched sides again, rejoining Pantsoff.

"Isn't someone going to pour me a drink?" said Pantsoff. The sun came up and turned the already motionless trolls to stone, as usual. Bulbo looked them over carefully and then rushed forward, wrapping his arms around Pantsoff's legs in fake gratitude.

"Pantsoff, thank heaven you've come! It was horrible. I tried to warn the dwarves, but—Hey, how did you do that? Get them arguing, I mean."

"Learn To Throw Your Voice!" Pantsoff said. "Amaze Your Friends! Baffle Your Enemies! The best Ten Easy Lessons I ever took."

The next thing was to unsack the dwarves. Fallin started criticizing Bulbo as soon as he was free.

"Somehow, I got the impression that you were making a deal with those trolls as I arrived," the dwarf said.

"Dealing? With trolls? Never! We Bunkinses have always been very hard-line on that sort of thing. No negotiation with trolls is our policy," said Bulbo.

"Then why were you shaking hands with them and laughing?"

"It just appeared that way. The trolls were planning on eating me. They weren't shaking my hand, they were seeing if I was young and meaty enough to make me into Osso Buco. They were laughing with delight at how well-marbled I looked!"

"Let's leave our consultant alone and focus on priorities," said Pantsoff. "Our highest priority is getting me an eye-opener—can someone mix up some Bloody Arwens?"

"Is whiskey good enough?" said Borin.

"Even better!"

"It's right over there by the fire. Help yourself to one of those very large jugs."

"Speaking of which," said Pantsoff. "Whatever happened to that Goblin Queen? Your grandfather really had a thing for her. Did he ever mention her to you, Borin?"

It's not easy to embarrass a dwarf, but Pantsoff had just embarrassed twelve of them. They looked at their boots, wishing they were still in sacks about to be eaten. They're hard to embarrass but easy to insult. Borin leapt up to attack Pantsoff.

"You know," said Pantsoff, "these trolls probably have a treasure hidden around here."

Borin stopped in his tracks. There was a moment of absolute silence.

All the dwarves looked at Pantsoff with great interest, all insults and embarrassment forgotten.

"Go on," said Borin, trying to sound casual.

"What, you mean the troll-loot?" said Pantsoff. "Oh, absolutely! Probably it's in that cave over there, behind the stone door."

Sure enough, there was a cave and a stone door. They all tried to push it open while Pantsoff relaxed nearby, speaking half-hearted incantations while he massaged his feet. But the door would not open.

"Would this help?" asked Bulbo. "I found it on the ground where the trolls had their fight." He held out a key, which was, of course, very large.

"Give me that!" snapped Pantsoff as he grabbed it from Bulbo's well-marbled hands. He fitted it into the key-hole, the stone door swung in with one big push, and they stepped in as Bulbo wondered aloud "How often do you have to paint a stone door?" He really wanted to upgrade from the aluminum screen door on the front of his hole.

The cave had bones on the floor and a nasty smell in the air. So nasty, in fact, that the dwarves and Pantsoff lit their pipes, which was an improvement. There was food jumbled carelessly on an ancient formica countertop along one wall. There were pots of gold in the corner. In another corner were personal items formerly belonging to various victims. Citing the ancient rule of "finders keepers" everyone helped themselves. Pantsoff and Borin each took an ostentatiously bejeweled sword. They were not Very Large, just regular sword-size.

"Look at these flashy blades!" said Pantsoff. He drew his sword and struck a dramatic pose. "Don't I look splendid?"

"Mine has runes on it, Pantsoff," said Borin. "Here, look at this."

"Ah, I see!" said Pantsoff, hesitantly. He took the blade and examined it closely. "Yes, yes. These are definitely runes." He handed the sword back to Borin.

"That's it? You can't translate it?"

"Borin, I can read all the languages of goblins, dwarves, elves and men. All of them, except the runes on that sword. And on my sword here. And this knife I found. Anything else, though," he said, glancing around the room to ensure there were no other runes present, "anything else, I can read."

"Let's get out of here," said Bulbo. "This is a smell you can't get used to."

They stepped back outside. Incredibly, they took some of the troll-food out of the foul cave, as well as the treasure. The artisan cheese and focaccia bread looked okay, especially after too many weeks on the road eating take-out food from Burger Steward and Southron Fried Chicken. But they had no interest in meat left behind by the trolls.

"It might be somebody we know," said Fatso, who was not normally so finicky.

They immediately drank the very large jugs of corn whiskey. Shortly before he passed out, Pantsoff wrinkled his nose. "What smells funny?" he asked, and then took out the knife with the runes, which he had quietly pocketed earlier.

He sniffed it carefully. "Great stinking elephants!" he exclaimed. "This thing still smells like that awful cave. Here, shorty, you keep it." He tossed it to Bulbo.

"My first paycheck," mumbled Bulbo. "Maybe if I wash it in tomato juice—"

Later that day, as their headaches and nausea began to ease off in the early evening, they buried the treasure very secretly under a large "X" near the cave. Pantsoff made a great show of placing many spells over it, to protect it until they returned. The dwarves enjoyed the incantations and flashes of light at the beginning, but grew impatient during

Pantsoff's card tricks at the end. Finally, they loaded the ponies and got underway.

They hiked for a good twenty minutes before stopping for dinner. After they ate the disgusting but satisfying troll-leftovers, Borin stood up.

"No more troll-cheese for me," Borin said. "I'm going to bed. Loin and Groin, have you put up my tent yet? I hope you've oiled it properly." He turned toward Pantsoff.

"Where did you go to, yesterday, if I may ask?" he said.

"Out," Pantsoff replied.

"And what did you do?" continued Borin.

"Nothing."

"What kind of answer is that?"

"I went on ahead," said Pantsoff, "to spy out our road and search for provisions. I finally do something to help, and now all you do is yell at me! Well, as I searched, I ran into a couple of old friends from The Hidden Valley Ranch And Resort.

"Where's that?" said Bulbo.

"Do you mind?" said Pantsoff. "I'm talking with Borin! As I was saying, I met two of Enron's people, and by people I mean elves. We had a few drinks, and they warned me about the trolls and gave me some coupons for the Hidden Valley buffet.

"We talked about the resort business for a while, but then my uncanny sixth sense told me I was wanted back. It's never failed me! And sure enough, there you were, thirteen dwarves in sacks, like the trolls had just bought you at some hideous supermarket. At least your consultant managed to stay out of trouble."

"Yes, but how, I wonder?" said Borin suspiciously, as he raised one extremely bushy eyebrow.

Chapter 3

REST STOP – 2 MILES

They did not sing or tell stories the next morning. They didn't even play improv games or do reader's theater. As soon as the sun came up the dwarves dismantled their massive, iron-bound pup tents. They were back on their tiny petting-zoo ponies in no time, dragging their feet closer and closer to a great mountain ahead of them.

"G-Gosh!" said Bulbo. "Is that *The* Mountain?" He was easily impressed.

"Bunkins, you've really got to get out once in a while," said Fallin. "At least look at a map. This is only the beginning of the terrible Moisty Mountains. We've got to climb through them somehow. And then find our way through a vast, dark, dangerous forest. And then we fight the dragon. Did I say 'we' on that last one? I meant 'you.'"

"O!" said Bulbo. He was so flummoxed that he left the "h" off his exclaimed "oh." This brought familiar feelings of pain from his sore lower back. Soon he was thinking of a beer and the La-Z-Boy in his studio apartment. Not for the last time!

Now Pantsoff led the way. Bulbo suspected that Pantsoff was just trying to bulk up his resume:

Project Manager and Team Leader of doomed adventure to kill Smog the Dragon; only surviving team member.

35

Pantsoff claimed he was trying to find a special, secret place where they'd be able to sleep in real beds for a few nights and eat food that wasn't cooked by trolls. On "spits."

A couple of the more foolish dwarves, Tori and Rori, made the mistake of appearing interested in what Pantsoff was talking about. Soon Pantsoff was describing the special, secret place in tedious detail.

"Somewhere ahead of us is the fair Hidden Valley Ranch, where Enron makes his famous Ranch Dressing. There he lives, in the fabulous Last Waffle House. I sent a message by my friends, and we are expected."

"They're Pantsoff's 'friends,'" said Borin quietly to Fallin. "So I'm sure they're super-reliable."

The home of Pantsoff's friend in the Hidden Valley was indeed secret, and difficult to find. Bulbo assumed that name "Hidden Valley" was mostly a marketing thing, but it turned out the valley was literally hidden.

They rode in circles for a while, lost. At one point Pantsoff wanted to go back to the troll camp and start over. Finally, they stopped so the ponies could eat some grass at one of the roadside grass stations. Fallin insisted that Borin ask the attendant for directions. Fortunately, the man had some Last Waffle House brochures. He gave them one that had a map and some valuable coupons.

They paid for the grass (the ponies ate many kilos), as well as for some candy to keep Loin and Groin from fussing, and then moved on. With the maps, they soon found a landmark. There were small stones painted grey that marked out a path. This path eventually led them to a huge, bright billboard that invited them to "Visit the Last Waffle House at the Hidden Valley Ranch! See the Singing Elves, famous throughout Little Earth!"

"I knew I was on the right track all along! Lead on, Buttercup!" Pantsoff said to his horse.

Hours later, the dwarves were hungry and cranky. Bulbo was thinking fondly of the troll leftovers. Pantsoff tried to act as if things were going as planned.

"Here it is at last!" he suddenly called out. The dwarves had heard him say that every twenty minutes since the billboard, so they ignored him at first. But after yet another "Great Elephants, I've done it again!" he pointed to a sign next to a gateway that read "Welcome to the Hidden Valley! Try our famous Ranch Dressing!" Through the gateway they went, following a narrow path.

Bulbo never forgot the terrifying way the path suddenly plummeted downward a few yards past the gate. "You wouldn't throw me, would you, Diablo?" he whispered in his pony's ear. Diablo remained silent. The wobbit wished he been better to the animal. He wondered if it held any grudges as it tippy-toed down the very steep and uneven path. Bulbo had secretly been eating its oats.

Wobbits are not afraid of heights, but they are deathly afraid of falling. This is the main reason they never use stepladders. It's also why they go barefoot.

Eventually, the path leveled off and they were passing through groves of shoe trees. They came to an open glade not far above the edge of a colorful water slide, which blocked their progress.

"Hmph. Smells like elves," thought Bulbo. "Or is that chlorine?" Just then there came a burst of song like laughter in the trees. The tune reminded Bulbo of "Sweet Molly Malone" if it were being sung at you by a group of taunting choreographers:

> O! What are you doing,
> And where are you going?
> Your courage needs screwing
> Your noses need blowing!
> > O! tra-la-la-lally
> > here down in the valley
> > Sing cockles and mussels
> > Alive, Alive-O!

> O! What are you seeking,
> And where are you making?
> Our faggots are reeking,
> Our muffins are baking!
> > O! tril-lil-lil-lolly
> > the valley is jolly
> > your ponies look cockeyed
> > but lively, heigh-ho!

> O! Where are you going

With luggage you're lugging?
Your beards all need mowing
Except Mister Bunkins
    O! tril-lil-lil-lolly
    Your project is folly
    You'll wish you were muscle-bound
    Singing heigh-ho!

O! Will you be staying
Or with the crows flying?
Which ten will live gaily
Which three will be dying?
    O! Stay here, by golly
    In our Hidden Valley
    All bearded and iron-bound
    Singing heigh-ho!

The singers were elves, of course, the Famous Singing Elves of The Hidden Valley Ranch And Resort. Bulbo loved elves, or at least he loved the idea of elves. He had never actually met one, or even seen one. He was a little frightened of them, as he was of almost everything.

Dwarves don't get on well with elves. Even decent enough dwarves think them foolish, which is understandable: consider the lyrics in that last song. Other dwarves, dwarves who have had their decency called into question publicly by bank regulators, dwarves like Borin, consider elves to be an unnatural threat to the order and profitability of Little Earth. This is because many elves criticized SmithiBank's 21-day check hold policy and its substantial overdraft penalties. Mostly, dwarves dislike when elves make fun of their beards.

"Well, well!" said a voice. "Just look! Bulbo the wobbit on a pony, my dear! Isn't it delicious!"

"What an odd remark!" said Bulbo quietly to Pantsoff, looking around uneasily. "Was that an elf? What does he mean by 'delicious?'"

"Bulbo!" said Pantsoff. "You're embarrassing me! We're not in Wobbiton anymore. Try to act sophisticated while we're staying with the elves, all right?"

Ignoring Bulbo, the elves went off into another song even more poorly-conceived than the one I have written down in full. At last one elf, a tall, slim, young, fine-featured fellow, came out from the trees and bowed to Pantsoff and to Borin.

"Welcome to the Hidden Valley Ranch!" he said.

"Thank you for coming out," said Borin, a bit awkwardly. Pantsoff had moved on, and was already having Buttercup valet-parked while chatting with some other, equally handsome elves.

"You are a little out of your way," said the elf, "that is, if you are making for the lonely path across our Water Slide and to the Waffle House beyond. We will set you right, but you had best check your ponies with the valet. Don't worry about tipping. Everything is included in your package. Are you going to try the water slide, or join us for karaoke, or go straight on? The Waffle And Salad bar will be open soon. I can smell the ranch dressing!"

Tired and sore-backed as he was, Bulbo would have liked to stay for a while. Elvish karaoke is not a thing to miss, not if you've had a couple mojitos and care for show tunes. He would have liked to share a few private words with these people. They had such slender builds, such contemporary hairstyles, such exquisite fashion sense. What was their secret, he wanted to know. And what did their women look like? He hadn't seen any yet, but he thought he would like to.

But the dwarves were all for supper as soon as possible and would not stay. They grudgingly turned over their little ponies, briefcases, brochures, golf bags, and paraphernalia to the valets, and walked to the bridge over the water slide. Predictably, the elves sang a merry song, which I'll spare you, as the party went across.

"Don't dip your beard in the water, father!" they said to Groin. "The chlorine might turn those fabulous highlights green!"

"Mind Bulbo doesn't eat all the waffles! Have him try our fat-free Ranch dressing on some salad instead!" they called. "He is too fat to crawl through any duct-work yet!"

"Hush, Hush! Good people!" said Pantsoff, meaning the elves. "Valleys have ears, shoes have tongues, and potatoes have eyes. Good night!"

And so they all came to the Last Waffle house, and found its lobby fully staffed.

Now it is a strange thing, but things that are good to have and days that are good to spend are not much to listen to, while things that are uncomfortable, palpitating, and even titillating may make a good tale. So although it's uninteresting, you should know that Borin & Company stayed a long time in that house, and found it hard to leave all the amenities, especially the turndown service with the mint on their pillow every night. They also liked the copy of Little Earth Today they received every morning.

Enron, the owner and manager, was an elf-friend—he had both Elves and Men as his ancestors. This made some of the dwarves uncomfortable. Anytime Borin wasn't in mixed company, he would grumble about the "half-elf" and use words like "miscegenation" and "octoroon." Pantsoff had to remind him "The valley has ears," and pointed at a decorative ear with a jeweled ear-cuff protruding from a nearby sconce. "Enron might hear you!"

Enron was as stylish and fair in face as an elf-lord, as chiseled as a warrior, as wise as a wizard, as shrewd as a dwarf tycoon, and as fair as a summer day. He comes into many tales more reputable than this one, where his part is small, but important, as you will see, if we ever get to the end of it. His waffle house was perfect, if a little expensive, whether you liked breakfast buffets, or spa treatments, or salsa lessons, or just sitting and staring at people in the lobby. Riff-raff did not come into that resort. It was too pricey.

Everyone had a lovely time. The ponies got better treatment than they had ever received from the dwarves or their previous masters at the petting zoo. The dwarves had their clothes tailored and they picked up a few new things as directed by wise elf haberdashers. Their coolers and thermoses were filled with snack bars and energy drinks, all free of transfats and sodium, yet high in protein and dietary fiber. Their plans, incomplete and improbable when Pantsoff first presented them, were improved with Enron's famous advice. They had a final meeting on Midsummer Eve. They were to go on again the next day, on Midsummer Morning, following a visit to the special Midsummer Build Your Own Waffle Bar.

Enron was at the meeting that night because he actually knew about things, especially runes. As he looked at the swords Borin and Pantsoff took from the troll's lair, he said, "These are very old swords. Classics. They don't make them like this any more. We used to stock a few of these in the Hidden Valley sword shop, The Swordatorium. But all they did was take up floor space. Too expensive for vacationers.

"The swords you two have are still valuable: they're used, their original packaging is lost, but they're in near-mint condition. No sloppy, stupid, thumb-fingered dwarf could have made these, no offense, Borin. They are obviously of elf-make. Just look at the timeless styling and clean lines. Borin, your sword is named Orcbriss, also called the Goblinator, the ancient chopper of many a goblin crotch. Yours, Pantsoff, is named MC Foehammer, also called Hamstring, the favored sword of the King of Gondola, who was himself a renowned cheap-shot artist. Keep them well!"

"Whence did the trolls get them, I wonder?" said Borin, as he mentally calculated the fair market value of his sword in comparison to its potential price at auction. "And how can I preserve its value? Should I have it professionally reconditioned, or should I just wrap it carefully and put in storage?"

"If I were you," said Enron, "I'd keep it handy, clean, and well-oiled. You're headed into the mountains, so you'll need it to keep the goblins away. And it'll glow if there are enemies nearby, but of course you have to have it drawn or you'll never notice. And you won't see the glow if you're in broad daylight, but then of course you'll be able to see your enemies anyway. The glow certainly looks nice. In any event, this is a better weapon than whatever blunt, bunged-up dwarf-built hatchet you might be using now."

Borin had reached his limit, but he decided to remain cordial until after settling his huge mini-bar bill. "Yes, well, we don't have any other swords than these that you see." He nodded towards Pantsoff. "It seems my project manager didn't include swords in our packing list."

"Really! Well, I'm sure Pantsoff knows what he's doing. Right, Pantsoff?" said Enron.

"All part of the plan, my friends," said Pantsoff. "Just trying to keep everyone on their toes and in the moment. Hate to over-prepare. But enough about me. Let's look at the map that I recovered." Pantsoff got out the map. Enron turned it over to the side with the maze and the connect-the-dots.

He took it and gazed long at it. The Midsummer Eve Moon was shining in a broad silver crescent. He held up the map and the white light shone through it. "This is a Moon Jumble," he said.

"A what?" asked the wobbit. He was more of a sudoku guy, but he thought a jumble might be handy later on. He was always looking for a way of killing time while Pantsoff was talking to him.

"Moon Jumbles are Rune Jumbles, and often also June Jumbles," said Enron. "You cannot complete the Jumble when you look straight at it. The moon has to shine through from behind. I believe it's a dwarf invention, isn't that right, Borin?"

Borin stared blankly back for a moment, still thinking about how to get the best price for his sword. He then realized he had been asked a question while he wasn't listening. This happened a lot. He used anger to bluff his way out, as usual. "Stop yammering and translate it!" he said. "What kind of resort is this?"

"It says 'Stand by the service entrance when the parrot knocks,'" read Enron "'and the setting sun with the last light of Derwin's Day will shine upon the key hole, unless it's cloudy.' What is Derwin's Day?"

"It's also called Dwarven Independence Day. It celebrates our hard-won independence from other, more wealthy dwarves."

"What?" said Bulbo again.

"You wouldn't understand. It's a dwarf thing." Borin said.

"It's settled, then," said Enron. "You have very little time. You're leaving tomorrow. Checkout is at 11:00. You'll get your bill tonight for our Express Checkout. If you order any room service, that will be charged separately. Your coupons are good for tomorrow's waffle-bar. Here's your map." With their meeting over, they all stopped in the cabaret to see the special Midsummer Eve Elf Floor Show.

Midsummer Morning came too quickly. Many waffles and gallons of whipped cream were consumed while the final amenities charges were being argued about. Eventually, the syrups and fixings and massive, iron-bound waffle-irons were taken away, despite the dwarves' complaints about the true meaning of "All you can eat." Disappointed, they sat down on their tiny ponies and rode away, toward the Moisty Mountains and the land beyond.

Chapter 4

OVER HILL, OVER DALE

Long days after they had climbed out of the Hidden
Valley and left the Last Waffle House miles behind, they
were still climbing up and up towards and then through the
mountains. It was a hard and dangerous path, largely because
of the "knowledge and memory" of Pantsoff. Despite
Pantsoff's protests, the dwarves and the wobbit used the wise
advice of Enron, and they eventually found the right road to
the right mountain pass. When a dwarf takes the advice of an
elf, or even a half-elf like Enron, you know that dwarf really
needs advice. Pantsoff continued to offer his own advice
freely.

From up in the Moisty Mountains they could look
down, back over the lands they had left, laid out far below.
Bulbo tried not to enjoy the view any more than necessary,
and then only if there was no chance of falling. Preferably
while sitting on the ground, with his arms around Fatso's
neck. Every so often, though, Bulbo would take these
precautions and dare himself to look. Far, far away in the
west, Bulbo knew that the hamlets and cutlets and towns back
home were still there. Bugford Falls, Bug Park, Bugger Forest
and even dear old Wobbiton itself were all still there. None of
them interesting, none of them exciting in the potentially
lethal way the adventure was. Entire villages of safe and
comfortable things, free of trolls and cliffs. How many copies
of the Wobbiton Shopper had accumulated in front of the
aluminum screen door to his dear little studio apartment?

He shivered. Bulbo never realized how bitterly cold it got high in the mountains, moisty or otherwise. He complained about the wind until the avalanches started, and then he complained about them. The nights were even colder and no one wanted to talk, except Pantsoff. The dwarves gave up singing. Bulbo tried to get them started on "Ninety Nine Flagons Of Ale On The Wall," or even "Heigh-Ho," but they felt uncomfortable breaking the library-like silence around them.

"Summer is getting on down below," thought Bulbo, "and sidewalk sales and five-furlong fun runs. They will be barbecuing and block-partying before we even go down the other side at this rate." And the others were thinking equally gloomy thoughts.

Not long before, they had said goodbye to Enron in the high hope of Midsummer Morning, thanks to the paraphernalia they had packed. They had thought of coming to the service entrance at One SmithiBank Plaza, "and perhaps it will be Derwin's Day." Then they all agreed that they would not exchange Derwin's Day gifts that year, because of the difficulty in shopping while on an adventure. At the time, this struck Bulbo as odd.

So there in the Moisty Mountains, Bulbo asked Borin, "When we left the Hidden Valley, you said 'Perhaps it will be Derwin's Day,' when we arrive at the Only Mountain. But didn't the Moon Jumble say that Derwin's Day was the only day we'd be able to unlock the service entrance? The only day we'd be able to find the keyhole for your key?"

"Quiet, Bunkins." Borin said. "There will be plenty of time to worry about the details later. We'll probably end up camped at the Mountain for weeks, patiently awaiting Derwin's Day. For now, leave me to my gloomy thoughts."

Pantsoff said nothing. He alone knew how weak his plan for the adventure actually was, and that this weak planning could become painfully obvious, quite literally, very soon.

Pantsoff knew there were any number of disasters that could occur as they passed over the mountains. One obvious danger was the local goblin mob. They had recently been multiplying like rabbits, and in some sad cases, with rabbits. There was a chance, however remote, that thirteen properly armed dwarves could turn away a goblin attack.

Unfortunately, most of the company still had no weapons at all. Their only weapons were the two swords and one knife they plundered from the troll camp. They could have bought swords back at the Hidden Valley, but they were a little overpriced in Borin's opinion.

Pantsoff had also left rain gear off the packing list. Some of the dwarves had golf umbrellas, but there was not a waterproof poncho among them. When most of your wardrobe is made of metal, as is the case with dwarves, getting caught in heavy rain can be a problem. Sure enough, one day they met a thunderstorm—more than a thunderstorm, a thunderbattle. It was as if a typhoon, a cyclone, a hurricane, and a blizzard were having a tag-team steel cage death match, with a tornado as referee.

Bulbo had never seen or imagined anything of the kind. He was able to find shelter under Groin's beard, but when he peeked out between the greasy braids, he saw that across the valley the stone giants were out, and they were hurling trolls at each other as a game. He soon stopped peeking, but could still hear the giants guffawing and shouting, and the occasional splat of an unlucky troll.

"This won't do at all!" said Borin. "Pretty soon they'll run out of trolls, and they'll use us to play Hacky Sack!"

"Well, if you know of anywhere better, lead us there!" said Pantsoff, who took criticism poorly.

Together, they decided to send Wheeli and Deali to look for a cave or a motel. They were young, and knew all the best places to vacation or dine. And they were expendable. Bulbo was expendable, too, but it would have taken four dwarves to get him out of Groin's beard, and sending two dwarves was more efficient. Borin thought of himself as efficient, despite a failed family business that proved otherwise.

Very, very soon Wheeli and Deali returned. "We have found a dry cave," they said, in unison, "not far around the next corner, between an old dark house and an abandoned summer camp."

"Have you completed your due diligence?" said Borin. "Performed a risk analysis? Checked for goblins?" He was very thorough when he wasn't doing the work.

Wheeli and Deali looked away for a moment, but then Pantsoff interrupted, "Yes, yes, whatever! I'm sure they did a great job, even though they didn't take much time at all. Another success! I've done it again! My instincts told me this was the best way through these mountains!"

Actually, it was Enron that told him this was the best way through these mountains, but the dwarves said nothing. They were all too busy running towards the cave. They immediately entered, each claiming a spot to lay down a massive, iron-bound sleeping bag. They even found room for the tiny ponies, all appropriately downhill from the rest of the company. In an attempt to look like a team player, the wizard lit up his wand so that a bluish light glowed from the end, a revolving one, much like you or I might see at K-Mart. He used this intermittent light to make a great show of checking the cave over, but all the while he was thinking about whether his leather hat would shrink while it dried.

Soon they were all smoking their terrible pipes. Bulbo got out a pipe he purchased at the Last Waffle House Smoke Shop, and joined in. He still thought the smell was disgusting, but it was nice to have a hobby. And dwarven peer pressure is a terrible thing.

Pantsoff entertained them with some magic, making various small personal items of theirs disappear. Then they talked and talked and talked, and so dropped off to sleep one by one. Pantsoff had first watch duty, so he had to stay awake until he was sure everyone else was asleep. And that was the last time the dwarves used their paraphernalia, as well as their briefcases, golf bags, brochures and ponies.

Everyone had suspected that the only reason Bulbo had been hired was to make Pantsoff look good by comparison. But that night in the cave, Bulbo started to establish his value to the dwarves. He could not go to sleep for a long while; and when he did finally sleep, he had very nasty dreams. Not nasty as in "Oooh, you nasty wobbit-boy." Nasty as in unpleasant. He dreamed he was back in school, taking an exam in a class that he had never attended before.

Of course, he was naked. Then he dreamed he was eating a giant marshmallow that tasted horrible.

At that, he woke up with a terrible start. His pillow was gone, and there were feathers in his mouth. Even worse, he woke to see the last of the ponies' tails disappearing into a black crack at the far end of the cave. "Someone really should have checked this place out more carefully," he thought, and then, realizing the seriousness of the situation, he shrieked.

Out jumped the goblins, big goblins. Bigger than Bulbo, at least, and almost the same size as Borin, but actually much smaller than Pantsoff. They were ugly looking, too, with their broken noses, slicked-back hair, and pinky rings. Out they jumped, before you could say *no running in the house*. There were two of them to each dwarf, although later accounts claimed as many as six. There was only one underachieving goblin for Bulbo. The entire company was grabbed and carried into the black crack before you could say *where's my coffee*. All except Pantsoff. When the goblins came to grab him, he gestured with his wand, then there was a terrific popping sound and a sweet, salty, buttery smell. Several of the goblins fell down dead, transformed into kettle-corn. Then Pantsoff vanished.

Bulbo and the dwarves were shoved through a doorway and a stone door closed behind them with a snap. Bulbo was thinking what an odd sound a "snap" was for a heavy stone door when he wondered: Where was Pantsoff? He wasn't surprised that Pantsoff had abandoned them again; in fact, he was starting to expect it. His disappointment in Pantsoff gave way to dread of the long, dark, twisting passage, and of the goblins themselves. The goblins were very rough, and they pinched unmercifully. To Bulbo, the pinching seemed gratuitous when everyone knew the goblins always enslaved or killed their captives. They also gave noogies, Indian wrist burns, and wet willies. They laughed their terrible mocking laughs, pausing only to say things like "Nobody's gonna see youse guys no more," and "Yer gonna sleep with the fishes!" Bulbo was even more unhappy than when he first met Borin. He wished again and again for a whiskey sour and his La-Z-Boy recliner. Not for the last time.

Now there came a glimmer of red light before them. The goblins began to sing, and like the dwarves, they had surprisingly good voices. The song itself reminded Bulbo of a traditional song he had sung when he was in a barbershop quartet, a favorite Dork pastime. The song was called Goodnight, Ladies. The goblin version was not as charming:

> *Goodnight, prisoners*
> *Goodnight, prisoners*
> *Goodnight, prisoners*
> *We're going to kill you all!*
>
> *Clap! Snap! Black crack!*
> *Grip, grab! Pinch-nab!*
> *Down now, my lad!*
> *Go down to Goblin-town!*
>
> *Swish, smack! Whip crack!*
> *Clash, crash! Crush-smash!*
> *Work, work! Don't shirk!*
> *'Cause first we'll enslave you all!*

It sounded truly terrifying, apart from the harmonies, which were quite lovely. Like you might see in an overly-literal music video from the eighties, the goblins took out whips and cracked them as they sang *Swish, smack!* With a whip behind him, even Borin hurried along, until they all stumbled into a large cavern.

It was lit by a low red fire in the middle, but otherwise it looked like a warehouse, and it was filled with goblins. They all laughed and stamped and slapped their hands, and they kept pinching, too. They especially liked pinching Bulbo, since he was by far the cutest of the company. Goblins were herding the ponies into a corner behind racks of expensive clothing, jewelry, wine, and fine tools. The sort of merchandise sold in the Hidden Valley, except it was all stolen. The briefcases, brochures and golf bags were laying broken open, being rummaged by goblins. Even worse, the paraphernalia was all over the place, being fingered by goblins, smelled by goblins, and smoked by goblins.

I am afraid that was the last they ever saw of those tiny, tiny ponies. The littlest one, the one that Bulbo rode, was being handed back and forth among the goblins, who each held it up to the light, admiring its fine coat and apparent juiciness. Since his horse was not suitable for the mountain passes, Enron had lent Pantsoff a jolly little sturdy white fellow, like a one-third scale miniature of Buttercup. The little fellow was looking less jolly and sturdy by the minute.

There in the shadows behind a large flat stone desk sat a tremendous goblin, almost Pantsoff's size, with a huge head, almost George Lopez's size. Armed goblins were standing around him, carrying the switchblades, garrotes and poisoned cannoli they commonly use. Now goblins are cheap, vengeful, and dishonest, but despite their similarities they don't get along with dwarves. They make no beautiful things: no ranch dressing or waffles or 30-year fixed mortgages, but they make many clever ones. Butterfly knives, blackjacks, water boards, and alligator clips they design very well, using outsourced labor to do the actual manufacturing. Their laborers work part time and without benefits until they die from poor lighting and repetitive stress syndrome. It is not unlikely that they have invented many things that have since troubled the world, such as payday loans, gossip tabloids and discount fireworks.

Goblins did not hate Dwarves especially, no more than everybody else did. But they had a hateful grudge against Borin's family, since SmithiBank had been making predatory loans and adopting usurious practices that were taking away the clients/victims that traditionally belonged to the goblins. With loan sharking compromised, the goblins were left only with bookmaking, gambling, protection, kidnapping, murder-for-hire, and prostitution. And goblin prostitutes had never enjoyed mass appeal. In any case, goblins don't care who they catch, as long as it's done quickly and cheaply, and the targets are weak, stupid, outnumbered or sound asleep.

"What am I to do with these fellows?" said the goblin behind the desk. His voice was quiet and raspy, with a slight lisp. "You cannot reason with them!"

"Yes, Gobfather," said one of the guards using the traditional term of respect for Agog, the king and spiritual father of the Moisty Mountain Goblins. "We asked them politely to identify themselves and explain their business, but they refused and ambushed us. Imagine, goblins attacked by unarmed, sleeping dwarves! Dwarves, and this wobbit," he pinched Bulbo, "defiling our Front Porch as if they owned the place!"

"Is this true?" said the Gobfather to Borin. He wore a mushroom in his lapel buttonhole, and took a moment to sniff it thoughtfully. "Why do you show such disrespect? First, you take away our legitimate lending business, and now this. I suppose you're friends with those *pezzonovante* elves, too. Come, now! What do you have to say for yourselves?"

"I am Borin, at your service," he replied. "We seek only shelter for the night."

"Hmm!" said the Gobfather. "And why does your business again conflict with mine? Why are you invading my home? I will soon know all about you, Borin Oakmanfield, although I already know more than I wish. The truth, now, or I'll have you stabbed, strangled and poisoned—in that order."

"There is no longer any conflict," said Borin. "Since the regulators closed down SmithiBank, my board of directors and I are pursuing other interests. We wish to spend more time with our families, on the other side of your scenic mountains."

"He's lying, Gobfather," said another of the guards. "Several of our people…

"People?" said Bulbo.

"Well, not people, you know, goblins," said the guard, "were magically transformed into popcorn when we invited the dwarves to meet with you. They were delicious, it's true, but they will be missed. Also, he has not explained this!" He dramatically held up a shovel. The Gobfather looked perplexed. "I mean, this!" He held up his other hand and brandished Orcbriss.

"Be careful with that, it's valuable!" Borin said, but the howling of the goblins drowned him out.

The Gobfather held his gigantic head and wept. "You come into my home, claiming innocence, while you carry this sword that has slain so many of my people, goblins, that is. This is Orcbriss, the chopper of so many fine, innocent goblin crotches during our defense against the unwarranted attacks by Gondola. I have no patience with elf-friends. Guards! Take them away! Make them comfortable, wait until they've relaxed and come to trust you, and then kill them suddenly! I'm sorry, Borin, but I have to do this. It's not personal, it's business."

A mob of goblins, some so huge they could see eye-to-eye with Borin the dwarf, stepped closer and closer. At the last possible moment, a voice rang out with grandiose theatricality "Look at me, everyone!"

All the goblins turned and looked to see Pantsoff in very dark glasses. Suddenly, there were bright, dazzling explosions all around him. In the low light of the cavern, the effect was completely confusing. "Typical Pantsoff," Bulbo thought.

Blinded by the flashes, the goblins all staggered around or fell over, like frat boys on spring break. A sword flashed in its own light and Bulbo heard Pantsoff yell "En garde, Agog!" as he attacked the Gobfather from behind. Agog looked down at the point sticking out of his chest and murmured "Mama Goblin, look at what they've done to your boy!" as he died. Realizing that their enemies had two swords among them, the goblins fled.

The sword went back into its sheath. "Fear not! I, Pantsoff, have come to rescue you! Follow me as we escape! Quickly, now, before the goblins build up the nerve to come after us. Me first!"

Borin grabbed his sword from the hand of the lifeless Gobfather and hustled to catch up with Pantsoff.

"Half a minute," said Rori. Bulbo owed him some money from when they played craps at the Hidden Valley Casino, and it would be hard to collect if Bulbo was dead. He made the wobbit scramble up on his shoulders and then they set off at a run, as if they were hurrying to a very important chicken fight.

They ran through the mountain like there were waffles at the far end. At the halfway point, Pantsoff stopped. He drew his sword, M.C. Foehammer, and held it aloft as it glowed, yelling "Ha-ha! Victory!" When he heard the sound of vengeful goblins approaching, he sheathed it again and lit up his wand in the dark passage. As the blue light flashed and flashed, he said "Is everybody here? Buddy up!"

Each dwarf found his buddy. Bulbo was Fatso's buddy, so the wobbit left Rori and climbed up onto Fatso's back instead. Before Fatso could complain, Pantsoff started congratulating himself again. "Just as I planned! Couldn't be better! By going through the mountain, we'll cut weeks off our trip! Let's go!" On they went, at a furious, goblin-induced pace.

"Why, oh why did I ever leave my studio apartment!" said Mr. Bunkins, bumping up and down on Fatso's back.

"Why, oh why did I put both whipped cream and butter on all those waffles!" said Fatso as he clutched at his chest. He staggered and fell over, and the wobbit dropped off his shoulders into the blackness of the tunnel. Bulbo bumped his head on a shovel, and remembered nothing more.

Chapter 5

RIDDLES WITH A DORK

When Bulbo opened his eyes, he wondered if he had, for it was just as dark with them shut. He didn't know where he was, or even who he was. For a moment he thought he might be a piece of bridge mix at the bottom of a very deep box. Then his sore back reminded him that he was Bulbo Bunkins from Wobbiton after all.

There were no goblins, no dwarves, not even Pantsoff. He groped about an all fours hoping to find his tiny pony. All he ended up finding was a small ring of cold metal lying on the floor. This was the turning point of his career, a resume-builder to say the least. As he held it, he heard terrible whisperings and was overcome with visions of a single, lidless, burning eye. These things he blamed on his hunger. He hadn't eaten since dinner yesterday, and it was now half-past brunch. He put the ring into a pocket of his vest, gave it a fussy little pat, and then thought about how hungry he was. He thought of himself frying gyros and eggs in his kitchenette at home.

After some time, even Bulbo became bored with thoughts of processed meat. He decided a smoke might be nice. It seemed somehow addictive. He felt for his pipe and leaf, and found both. Then he felt for a match, but found none. He was devastated, but then he came upon his little knife.

He drew it out. It still smelled like the troll cave. "Maybe some rubbing alcohol and a wire brush would fix that," he thought. He opened the main blade, and it shone pale and dim before his eyes.

"So it is an elvish blade, too," he thought, "and goblins are not very near, yet not far enough."

But somehow he was comforted. It was rather splendid to be carrying a pocketknife made in Gondola for the Elf Army of old. In addition to the main blade, it had many other blades and tools.

"Perfect!" he thought. "If I need to open a can of Elf Boyardee Ravioli, I'm all set. If only I had a can of ravioli!" The can opener looked crusty and smelled especially bad. "What did those trolls do with this knife?"

With nothing else to do, he held his Elf Army Knife in front of him with the main blade out, and began looking for an exit. Or a can of ravioli.

*   *   *

Bulbo found no cans of ravioli, or anything else. He walked on and on in the dark, which is no joke if you're barefoot. Bulbo couldn't even walk from his bed to his bathroom in the dark without stubbing his toe at least once, so you can imagine how unhappy his walk through the cave was. He stepped on and into a great many things that would cause you or me to leave our shoes on the porch for a while, so when he stepped into some cold water, it was a nice change of pace. There was an echoey dripping sound which made Bulbo think he was near a dwarf's nose.

He looked for Borin & Company, but discovered instead that he was standing in the shallow end of a subterranean lake. Most of the wobbits on the Dork side of Bulbo's family were poor swimmers, since they were discouraged from participating in gym class as youths. Bulbo was no exception, so he decided not to wade any deeper. Which was wise.

Deep down by the dark water lived old Gol-Gol, a small, wobbit-sized, slimy creature. I don't know where he came from, or who or what he was, but I'll try to make something up if I write any sequels. He was thin, with two big round eyes that glowed palely in his skinny face, sort of like a supermodel. That may be why his friends, back when he had friends, used to call him Lady Gol-Gol. He had a little boat that was big enough only for him, which may explain his current lack of friends. With his Size 14 feet he quietly paddled about, looking for fish. He grabbed these with his long, supermodel fingers, thus saving money on bait. Fish was almost all he ate, but he ate goblin, too, when he could get it. He was better at strangling from behind than any goblin. Being able to strangle at a better-than-goblin level is a real accomplishment.

Lady Gol-Gol lived on a slimy island of rock in the middle of the lake, which was also slimy. He watched Bulbo from his island, peering through the dark with his big luminous supermodel eyes. He could see that Bulbo was no goblin, which Bulbo would have considered a nice compliment, had he only known.

Gol-Gol got into his slimy boat and shot off from the island while Bulbo was sitting flummoxed and bebothered. He landed silently and got quite close before Bulbo looked up, flummoxed but no longer bebothered. With strangling from behind out of the question for the moment, Gol-Gol spoke. His voice was surprisingly loud and brash, utterly at odds with his appearance.

"Bless us, I say, bless us and splash us, my precious!" Gol-Gol bellowed. "Looky here! This boy'd make a tasty morsel, I say, a tasty morsel!"

"Who are you?" Bulbo said, thrusting his knife in front of him. With his glowing eyes, his bellowing, and his talk of eating Bulbo, Gol-Gol hadn't made a very good first impression.

"Who am I? The question is," Gol-Gol thundered, while poking Bulbo in the chest, "who are you?" He was really enjoying having someone to speak with, although the conversation was habitually one-sided.

"I am Mr. Bulbo Bunkins. I have lost my dwarves and I have lost my wizard, and I'm looking for the nearest exit that's unguarded by goblins."

"What's that, I say, what's that in your hand, boy?" said Gol-Gol. "A fish? A rock? Out with it, boy, out with it!"

"An Elf Army Knife, which came out of Gondola!"

"Well now," said Gol-Gol. "That's a fish of a different color!" Gol-Gol had never found himself at the business end of a glowing magic elf weapon. As a show of respect, he stopped poking Bulbo's chest and put his arm around Bulbo's shoulders instead. His voice remained loud and insistent.

"The name's Gol-Gol. Listen here, boy, I have an idea. Why don't you and I chat for a bit, you know, visit! Chew the fat. Look at me when I'm talking to you, boy! Now, how about a few riddles?" Gol-Gol wanted to appear friendly until he could figure out how to throttle Bulbo without getting stabbed. He was also trying to decide if he should eat Bulbo with a side of sushi, or ceviche, or sashimi.

"Very well," said Bulbo, who was anxious to agree, at least until he could figure out a way of stabbing Gol-Gol in the back. He was concerned that, even though Gol-Gol was carrying no visible weapon, he might know hypnosis or bleed acid or have razor-sharp elbows. Coincidentally, since Bulbo hadn't eaten for days, he was starting to wonder if Gol-Gol might be palatable, perhaps if prepared with the right sort of marinade.

"You ask first," he said. Bulbo was trying to recall a riddle, any riddle, but all he could come up with were limericks.

So Gol-Gol blustered out:

> *How, I say, how do you know*
> *If there's a dragon in your kitchen?*

"Easy," said Bulbo, who spent a lot of time in the kitchen. "Look for its footprints in the butter!" Bulbo's answer was right.

"This boy's smarter than he looks, but that ain't saying much," Gol-Gol said loudly to himself. Centuries of solitude had messed up his internal dialogue.

"Boy, I say, boy! If that riddle was so easy, let's have us a little competition, then. And just to make it interesting, you know, up the ante, let's agree that if I ask and you don't answer, I'll eat you. If you ask me and I don't answer, I'll show you the way out." Bulbo was speechless at how ridiculous Gol-Gol's proposal was. Did Gol-Gol really expect

Bulbo to allow himself to be eaten if he lost the game? "Well? Speak up, boy!"

"All right!" said Bulbo, using the game to buy time until he could come up with a plan. It was his turn, and he had to think of a riddle. He tried to ignore all the great knock-knock jokes he was suddenly remembering, and focus on a riddle. Finally, he thought of one.

> What's black and white
> And red all over?

"I know!" shouted Gol-Gol. "A half-eaten Zebra fish! No, wait, a newspaper! That's it! A newspaper!" He was correct.

"My turn!"

> What's green and red
> And goes fifty-five miles per hour?

Fortunately for Bulbo, this riddle was almost the same as his. He quickly gave the correct answer, which was "A frog in a blender." He was beginning to see how Gol-Gol's mind worked, as far as that goes. He thought Gol-Gol might be stumped by a riddle about life above ground.

> What's yellow
> And goes "Click, click, click?"

"This boy's about as sharp as a bowling ball," Gol-Gol said in a loud aside to himself. "Why, a ball-point banana, of course!"

Gol-Gol had answered correctly again, but thoughts of bananas, bloody fish and pureed frogs were making him hungry. It was having the same effect on Bulbo, but Bulbo didn't have a history of eating creatures that could talk with him, except parrots, of course. Gol-Gol thought and thought, and could only come up with a food-related riddle, but it was one that he considered quite difficult. He hadn't heard it in many, many years:

Why did the chicken
Cross the road?

Unlike Gol-Gol, Bulbo had memories of chickens, roads, and the riddle itself that were not centuries-old. He quickly answered "To get to the other side," as easily as you or I might.

Bulbo didn't intend to ask another food riddle, either. He suspected that Gol-Gol was admiring his excellent marbling, and he would have liked to change the subject. But the only riddle he could come up with was:

Why did the elephant
Sit on the marshmallow?

Gol-Gol had a hard time with this one. "Marshmallows? Elephants? What the, I say, what the heck are you talking about, boy? There's something odd about a boy that asks a riddle like that. Now, let's see—Oh! I know this one! The elephant sat on the marshmallow to keep from falling into the hot chocolate! Ha!"

He was right, and Bulbo wondered briefly if Gol-Gol remembered more about the outside world than he let on. Then Gol-Gol spoke up:

Why do firemen
Wear red suspenders?

Now Bulbo preferred belts rather than suspenders, and there were no firemen in his family, at least, not on the Dork side. As for Gol-Gol, he kept up his centuries-old tattered pants with a slimy piece of string. So Bulbo was truly taken off guard. He stalled for a moment, and then noticed Gol-Gol flipping through a book titled <u>To Serve Wobbits</u>. This snapped him back to reality and he was able to come up with the correct answer.

"They wear red suspenders to keep their pants up!" Bulbo said. He knew his next riddle would make Gol-Gol think of eating once again, but he couldn't think of anything else:

What did the snail
Say to the police
When he was robbed
By two turtles?

"Turtles and snails!" Gol-Gol bellowed. "There you go again, boy, asking me another tasty food riddle! Say, that reminds me of when my old granny and me used to rob snails by the riverbank. Now, what would a snail say if he wasn't eaten by me, but robbed by some turtles instead? I got it! He'd say 'Officer, it all happened so fast!' Ha!" Gol-Gol was right again.

"So let me ask you a tasty riddle, then:"

What did the snail say
When riding on the turtle's back?

Bulbo had no idea. He thought fleetingly of engaging Gol-Gol in a fair fight instead of answering. A fair fight in which Gol-Gol would be unarmed and Bulbo had a magic elf-weapon. Still, Bulbo didn't like the odds, and he had, after all, agreed to the riddle game. He was about to turn and run when a fish jumped out of the lake and landed, slimy and gasping, on Bulbo's bare feet. Startled, disgusted, and highly stressed, Bulbo screamed his little-girl-sounding Dork family scream.

"EEEE!" Bulbo screamed.

As luck would have it, that scream sounded enough like the riddle's answer for Gol-Gol to give him credit for being right. For, as you certainly know, a snail riding on a turtle's back usually says "WHEE!"

Gol-Gol was hungry, angry, and disappointed. But he tried to remain patient with Bulbo, who was having trouble coming up with another riddle. It seemed that Bulbo was about to lose the game.

"Come on, boy!" Gol-Gol said. "Don't stand there gawking! Out with it!"

Bulbo held his knife before him, and with his other hand checked his pockets, hoping to find a larger, more dangerous weapon. All he found was the gold ring he had

60

picked up in the tunnel. But he had forgotten all about it, and didn't even remember that it was there, or what it was. Reflexively, he asked aloud:

What have I got
In my pockets?

He was talking to himself, of course, but he got lucky once again. Gol-Gol thought Bulbo's inadvertent remark was a riddle! Gol-Gol may have been confused by the italics and the line break.

"What's the big idea!" said Gol-Gol, truly threatening despite his short, scrawny build. "That ain't no riddle! That's more of a trivia question!"

But Bulbo realized his good luck and decided to stick with it.

"You mean there are rules for this?" he said. "Come on! Answer the riddle! What have I got in my pocketses, I mean, pockets?"

"Well, if you say so," said Gol-Gol. "But gimme three guesses, then."

"Sure, whatever," said Bulbo. "Guess away." He couldn't believe Gol-Gol was okay with this.

Gol-Gol guessed all the things he kept in his pockets.

"Fish!"

"No."

"Rocks!"

"Nope."

"Slime, or maybe a shopping list!"

"Both wrong," said Bulbo, "and no double guesses. I win, and you have to show me to the nearest exit."

"Of course, son, of course," said Gol-Gol. "But first tell me, what have you got in your pockets?"

"Never you mind! Just take me to the exit." For some reason, Bulbo knew he shouldn't mention the simple ring that he found. For some other more mysterious reason, Gol-Gol didn't pursue the matter.

"Fine, son. Have it your way. But first," said Gol-Gol, chuckling to himself loudly, "let me go back to my island. I forgot to close the windows."

Bulbo rolled his eyes. "Okay, just hurry, will you?"

Gol-Gol paddled back to his island with his big flappy feet. There he kept a few slimy, wretched belongings: theater ticket stubs, old eyeglasses, forgotten business cards, breath mints, stray shirt buttons, foreign pennies, fish, and rocks. He also kept one very beautiful thing. A suspiciously simple golden ring—a precious ring.

"That boy wants my birthday present, but it's mine, all mine!" Gol-Gol said, with a deep, maniacal chuckle. "My magic ring! As soon as I find it, I'll slip it on my long, bony finger and I'll be invisible, I say, invisible! And then, after a little sneaky strangling, it'll be some tasty Wobbit Tartare for old Gol-Gol! I'm getting mighty tired of eating just fish and goblins. Now, where is that ring..."

Bulbo waited, tapping his foot, drumming his fingers, and looking around casually in the darkness. It was very dark without the light from Gol-Gol's luminous eyes.

Suddenly, Bulbo heard a screech. It was Gol-Gol, and he sounded really angry.

"Where, I say, where is it!" howled Gol-Gol. "Where in tarnation is my birthday present?"

"Your what?" Bulbo called back.

"Mind your own business, son. Where is it?"

"Look, I need to get going," said Bulbo. "You never answered my last riddle, and you said you'd take me to an exit. And not eat me. Come on!"

Gol-Gol was silent for a moment.

"Say, son, that reminds me," said Gol-Gol. "What's the answer to your riddle? What have you got in your little old pockets?" Gol-Gol got back into his boat. He starting paddling from his island towards Bulbo.

"I don't have time for this!" said Bulbo. "Let's go!"

"Certainly, son, certainly." Gol-Gol said as he paddled. "But first tell me, what have you got in those little old pockets?"

"Sure. Fine. I'll tell you, but first you tell me what you've lost." Bulbo was sure the lost item was either a fish or a rock, but he was starting, ever so slowly, to sense trouble.

"No. You tell me first."

"No, you first."

"No, you."

"No, you."

By this time, Gol-Gol had reached the edge of the lake. Bulbo didn't like where the discussion was headed, so he suddenly turned around and ran for it.

From behind, Bulbo could hear the flap of Gol-Gol's pursuing feet, his low, insane chuckle and the words "Just what have you got in those little old pockets?"

"What have I got in my pocketses?" Bulbo wondered as he panted and stumbled along in the dark, his knife still in his hand. He put his other hand in his pocket and the cold ring slipped onto his finger. He ignored the swooning sensation that came over him, as well as the sound, probably imagined, of an evil, grating voice chanting in an alien language.

Gol-Gol's crazy laugh sounded even closer. Bulbo turned and saw the huge glowing eyes. Then he stubbed his toe on a bucket of rocks. The rocks spilled out, he tripped on them, and fell.

In a moment, Gol-Gol was on him. Before Bulbo was able to beg for mercy or betray his absent friends, Gol-Gol passed by. He took no notice of Bulbo at all.

Bulbo was confused, but not flummoxed or bebothered. He guessed that Gol-Gol could see in the dark. Bulbo could still see the light from Gol-Gol's eyes as he headed down the tunnel, like watching a subway train leave the station. The light was bright enough that Bulbo could see some forgotten pickaxes further down the tunnel. How had Gol-Gol not seen him?

"I knew, I say, I knew it!" he heard Gol-Gol say. "The boy's gone and found my birthday present. Why, with my ring on his finger, any nincompoop could become invisible, secretly follow me to the exit, slip past the guards unseen, and escape!"

Gol-Gol's off-handed remark to himself contained enough detail to inform and encourage even Bulbo, who had almost given up on escape. He had been starting to make plans to become the new Lady Gol-Gol of the Moisty Mountains. But now that he knew the ring made him invisible, he could aspire to greater things, like escape and

63

repatriation to Wobbiton, perhaps via the Hidden Valley and Enron. But why was Gol-Gol heading towards an exit?

"Maybe," said Gol-Gol, "I'll be able to hear or smell the boy if I wait by the exit! I'll pay close attention, and when that dim-wit gives himself away with a footstep or a burp, I'll get my birthday present back and be done with my shopping for dinner as well! I can't wait! Off I go, to the Back Door!" He went on his way, muttering and laughing. Bulbo saw him come to a stop just past a shovel and a pile of debris.

"I'll wait, I say, I'll wait here," he said. "There'll be goblins to deal with if I go any further." Gol-Gol blocked the hall, putting one hand out and leaning on the passage wall.

Bulbo knew there would be no sneaking past Gol-Gol. He could certainly move without making a noise, but he couldn't move without making a smell. He hadn't had a bath since his last hot-tubbing at the Hidden Valley, and he had become understandably ripe since then. Certainly Gol-Gol would smell him if he tried to sneak by. He could stab Gol-Gol invisibly with his Elf Army Knife, or perhaps corkscrew him, but if Gol-Gol died slowly he might be able to strike back. Bulbo wanted to attack from behind, but could see no way to do it.

He noticed the stray shovel in the glow from Gol-Gol's eyes and knew what to do. Bulbo stepped forward, picked up the shovel, and faster than you could say *Why is that shovel floating towards me, and what's that smell?* he hit Gol-Gol with it. Gol-Gol stood dazed for a moment and then said "Down I go," as he fell. Bulbo skipped gingerly over him and turned the corner.

There he saw sunlight, an open door, and goblins. They were talking about all the recent excitement.

"If that wobbit comes this way, I'm gonna exterminate him!" said one goblin as he patted his sword-length switchblade.

"You better!" said the other, his captain. Bulbo could guess at their rank by the relative sizes of their pinky rings. "If you don't, I'm gonna exterminate you!" They laughed, and then both looked directly at Bulbo.

Magic Invisibility Rings are tricky things. You never know exactly how "invisible" you're going to become until you've had a chance to really test the ring using a full range of variables. For example, Bulbo's ring made him invisible, as well as his clothes, but with other rings, your clothes might remain visible, which is inconvenient and can lead to cold, embarrassing predicaments. Unfortunately, Bulbo didn't realize until it was too late that the shovel he was still carrying was entirely visible. He could clearly see the image of Gol-Gol's face stamped into it.

With his shocked realization of the shovel's visibility, Bulbo threw it away like a glob of hair from the shower drain. Then he ran straight at the goblins, counting on the element of surprise to give him the advantage. The goblins, on the other hand, charged directly at the shovel, their only visible enemy. As they chopped the shovel to bits, Bulbo ran out the door. But as Bulbo escaped, he heard Gol-Gol's cry echo up from the depths:

"Carn sarn it! Bunkins! We hates, I say, we hates it forever!"

Chapter 6

I ORDERED MY ENTREE FRIED,
NOT BROILED

The good news was that Bulbo had escaped the goblins and Lady Gol-Gol. Also, he was rid of Borin and Pantsoff, which wasn't exactly good news, but he didn't really miss them, either. Borin was always happy to tell everyone where to go, and what to stick where. But without Borin, Bulbo now had no map and no guide, which was bad news.

"What a disaster!" Bulbo said to himself as he walked away from the mountains. "I'd better get as far from the mountains and the goblins as possible. Maybe this road leads back towards the Last Waffle House. I could get a job at their espresso bar, I guess. I wonder if I'm stylish enough?" He looked back at the mountains sadly.

"Goodbye, mountains! Goodbye, failed adventure! Goodbye, treasure hoard and early retirement!" He then realized the sun was sinking westwards –*behind the mountains*.

"Good heavens!" he exclaimed. "I seem to have got right to the other side of the Moisty Mountains, right to the edge of the Land Beyond, and halfway to Nowheresville. There's no way I can get back through the mountains to Enron's place. Where could Pantsoff and the dwarves have got to? He's probably off crashing a company picnic, and they've probably gone where nobody knows them, to start a new bank!"

Bulbo then realized that they all might still be in the mountain, looking for the Back Door, or trying to rescue him, or perhaps being recaptured by the goblins. Then he thought that they were probably fine, just fine. Even though he had a magic weapon and a ring that made him invisible, it seemed pointless and foolhardy to go back to rescue his friends. Friends! He hadn't met any of them until just a few months ago. Then they insulted him, trashed his home, kidnapped him, and expected him to break into their offices and kill a dragon. Some friends! He was starting to congratulate himself for finally seeing his situation clearly when he heard voices.

He listened for a while, and then knew the voices weren't from goblins because he heard no discussion of putting a horse's head in anyone's bed. Whoever was talking might be willing to help him, but on the other hand, they might be just as happy to eat him. Bulbo quietly crept up closer to find out. The voices were coming from a dell by the road, near some hillocks and a glen or two.

Then he saw someone on lookout duty, peeking out of the dell. It was Deali, and he was looking directly at Bulbo. Bulbo realized he still had his ring on, so he decided to have some fun at Deali's expense. He was about to tie Deali's bootlaces together when a few words from the discussion in the dell caught his attention. It appeared to be a meeting to decide what to do about the missing Bulbo.

"It is resolved, then," said Borin. "We have unanimously decided to abandon Bulbo to the goblins or whatever end awaits him. We will honor him by splitting his share of the treasure amongst ourselves."

"I knew it!" thought Bulbo.

"Pantsoff," said Borin, "what is your backup plan for sneaking into our offices and killing the dragon?"

Pantsoff suddenly realized that his Plan B was even more incomplete that his Plan A. He had to change the subject, and fast.

"I know I voted to leave Bulbo to certain death like the rest of you, but now I have some regrets. I feel I may have been somehow responsible for the little fellow's predicament.

"Of course you feel responsible!" said Borin. "It was all your fault! You insisted that we bring him as a consultant, you did the faulty review of the cave where he was captured, you made him Fatso's buddy under the Buddy System!"

"Really!" said Pantsoff. "And I suppose I told Fatso to have a heart attack and drop him!"

"It wasn't a heart attack!" said Fatso. "It was acute angina. And why couldn't he run away on his own instead of being carried?

"Rori started it!" said Pantsoff.

"I carried him because he owed me some money, that's all," said Rori.

"He owes most of the rest of us, too," said Fallin. "We considered carrying him a 'bailout.' But now he's enslaved or dead or eaten, so we'll never get paid back. Look, this is a financial loss for all of us, but it's time to move on. Bulbo would have done the same for us."

"That's true," thought Bulbo.

"Well put, Fallin," said Borin. "Bulbo's share of the treasure will be distributed to offset all our losses from his unpaid debts. Now we just need to figure out how to kill the dragon, since our consultant is dead."

"I got your consultant right here!" said Bulbo, stepping down into the middle of them and slipping off his ring.

Bless me, how they jumped! Deali was quickly accused of sleeping while on look-out. Borin, who wasn't good at Succession Planning, was relieved that they were going back to Plan A, however flawed. Fatso clutched at his chest. But they all had to agree that Bulbo was, indeed, a skilled burglar. How else could he sneak up on them so cleverly? Bulbo saw no need to mention the ring yet. But he did tell them about his adventure and escape.

"There I was! All alone, with goblins, dozens of angry goblins, chasing me! My night vision is extraordinary, and I'm very fast going through tunnels, so I lost them soon enough. Then I was attacked by a monster named Gol-Gol! He was twenty feet tall and wreathed with flames. He had a whip and a sword and great wings, although he couldn't fly for some reason. Gol-Gol was going to eat me, but I tricked him into playing a riddle-game with me instead. Of course, I was the riddle-game champion of Wobbiton, so I won and Gol-Gol had to show me the way out. But he double-crossed me, so I slipped a finger into my stolen ring of invisi— I mean, I slipped past him silently, and right into twenty or thirty goblins guarding the Back Door! So I crept up on them, just like I did with you guys. I used the element of surprise, and killed a few of them with a shovel. I was able to escape in all the confusion, and here I am!"

"What did I tell you?" said Pantsoff. "Mr. Bunkins turned out to be a regular *Ringer*, didn't you, Bulbo?" Looking over his bushy moustache, he gave Bulbo one of those queer looks that Dorks are all accustomed to. Bulbo wondered what Pantsoff actually knew, or if he was just acting up for dramatic effect.

He didn't have long to wonder, though, because Pantsoff was soon getting Bulbo caught up on the dwarves' escape from the mountain. As before, he claimed that everything that happened was part of his secret master plan. He knew the cave was the goblin's Front Porch, he allowed them to capture the company and he arranged the escape, all to speed them through the Moisty Mountains from the inside.

"I doubt," said Pantsoff, "that Enron's advice could ever have gotten us so far, so quickly."

"So what!" said Borin. "Those goblins almost killed me!"

"Almost, but they didn't!" said Pantsoff. "Quite the contrary! I personally killed the Gobfather himself in single combat with my splendid new sword, Hamstring!"

"Single combat?" said Fallin. "He never saw you coming! You stabbed him in the back!"

"Thus I am avenged upon Agog The Goblin King for the humiliation I suffered alongside Borin's grandfather. 'Get your hands off my wife' indeed! Revenge is a dish that is best served *en brochette*!" Pantsoff had thought that line up hours ago, and was delighted to have a chance to say it.

"And I hope you all enjoyed the magic light show!" he said. As you remember, Pantsoff was famous for his legendary Magic Lights And Popcorn Spectacular, performed year after year at the Old Dork's Midsummer Eve party.

"It was great," said Borin, "so please tell us your plan for what's next! I'm especially curious about the replacement of our very expensive ponies, briefcases, brochures, golf bags, and paraphernalia."

"And what about food? I'm starving!" said Bulbo. For a moment, he thought Tori had transformed into a roast turkey. He was stepping forward to bite Tori's leg when Pantsoff intervened.

"Your questions will all be answered soon enough," said Pantsoff. "As Project Manager, I'll provide you with some proprietary information in due time. It is currently being provided on a need-to-know basis only. And now, Onward!"

With much grumbling, they went on. And on. And on. Evening came as they followed the road into a wood of pines. The sun set and they kept marching on.

"Pantsoff, can't we stop to eat, or sleep, or both?" said Bulbo.

"Absolutely!" said Pantsoff. "We'll stop at the first restaurant we see. And if they rent rooms, we'll stay for the night, too. Before bed we'll all go to the pool and play Orco Polo. Too bad we're still in the goblins' neighborhood where there are no restaurants or motels."

After much more walking, they came to a large clearing. The moon was up and shining brightly enough to get a good look around. Everything looked fine, just as the goblin's Front Porch had also looked fine. The clearing, however, somehow struck all of them as a dangerous, evil place. All of them except Pantsoff.

"Perfect!" he said. "We'll stop here for the night, and look for breakfast in the morning. I've found us the safest campground for miles. Rest easy, boys!"

At that moment, they heard a long, shuddering howl. Pantsoff smiled.

"No problem," he said. "That's probably just a stray dog."

The howling continued, and increased.

"Maybe a few coyotes, that's all. Once we get a fire going, they'll clear off."

Still more howling, and closer now.

"You know," said Pantsoff, "those might be wolves, but they're actually more afraid of us than we are of them."

Bulbo had been frightened at the possibility of a stray dog near their camp. With the threat level upgraded to multiple wolves, he was panicking.

"What shall we do, what shall we do!" he cried. "Escaping goblins to be eaten by wolves!" he said, and the saying caught on, though now we say "D'oh!"

"I see them," said Fallin, "and you're right, they're not wolves."

"I knew it!" said Pantsoff. "What are they? Foxes?"

"They're rargs!" said Fallin, as he climbed up a tree. The rest of the company was also climbing trees, except for Bulbo, who was climbing up Tori's back, while Tori climbed a tree.

"What's a rarg?" said Bulbo into Tori's ear.

"Do you mind?" said Tori. "It's not easy to climb a tree with a consultant on your back." That saying also caught on, though now we say "Eat my shorts, man."

Bulbo soon found out all about rargs. A rarg is like a wolf, only much, much worse. If a wolf and a shark had a baby that was raised by bikers, and later kidnapped and brainwashed by a satanic cult, it would be like a rarg. A number of them entered the clearing.

Vicious and evil though they are, Rargs cannot climb trees, nor can they fly up and spit venom. So they waited patiently at the foot of the trees, since dwarves were known to sometimes throw down one of their own as a bribe.

The glade was evidently a meeting place for the rargs. There appeared to be a big meeting planned tonight, perhaps to give out awards from a sales contest.

More and more rargs kept coming. Finally their chief arrived. The rargs sniffed each other's butts and then they sat down to listen to their chief start the meeting. He spoke to them in the dreadful language of the rargs.

"Rokay reverybody, ret's begin" said the chief. He went on to review the agenda for the evening, and then he read the minutes from their last meeting. Then he gave an update on their plans for a secret attack on a village of woodsmen and their families that was supposed to take place later that night. There would be refreshments afterwards.

"Ree-hee-hee!" laughed the rargs, as they cruelly licked their lips.

The chief continued by noting that the planned attack was to be part of a joint effort with the Moisty Mountain

Goblins, creating synergy and a new paradigm for viciousness.

"Ro boy o boy o boy!" said the rargs.

Then the chief explained that the goblins were running late because of the escape of some captives that murdered their Gobfather. Unfortunately, there would be no village attack tonight.

"Rut-ro!" said the rargs.

The chief concluded by pointing out that the goblin's runaway captives were hiding in the very trees that formed the roof of their meeting place. He then assured them that all was well. The goblins would arrive soon, kill the escapees, and feed them to the rargs. The attack on the woodsmen and their families would be re-scheduled to next week.

"Rooby roo!" cried the rargs in evil excitement.

The Company was soon dreadfully afraid, including Pantsoff, self-deluded charlatan though he was. But being ever the showman, he prepared some of his best magic so he could go out with a bang, perhaps literally.

"Watch this, everyone!" he said, as he tore a strip of bark off the tree and held it aloft. It suddenly rocketed out of his hand, trailing red sparks.

"Ooooo!" said the company from the trees.

The bark shot down towards a rarg, and exploded in white, with blue sparks.

"Ahhhh!" said the dwarves.

Pantsoff pulled off another strip of bark. This one shrieked as it took off in a blaze of yellow. As before, it exploded a rarg, but this one sparkled in green afterwards. Bulbo and the dwarves cheered.

Pantsoff shot another one at the rarg chief, who dodged behind one of his clan members. The unsuspecting rarg in front exploded with a white flash and a deafening boom. Polite applause came from the trees. Soon many of the rargs were either exploded or burning, which did nothing to improve their naturally evil mood.

* * *

"What in the world is going on down there?" said the King Of The Eagles. He was perched on a lonely pinnacle of rock on the east edge of the Moisty Mountains.

"Are the rargs having another party? Since when do they have fireworks? They must have invited the goblins."

The King Of The Eagles swept up into the air, accompanied by two of his court: the Prince Of The Eagles and The Duke Of The Eagles. With their far-seeing "eagle eyes" they could see flashes far below. They couldn't see the rargs, but they could hear their cries of "Rouch!" echoing up out of the wood. Also they could see the glint of the moon on the brass knuckles of long lines of approaching goblin button-men, enforcers and leg-breakers.

Eagles don't care about dwarves much one way or another, since they have limited banking needs and conduct most of their business on a "cash-only" basis. But they really hated goblins: their constant parties, their loud stupid music, and their non-stop outdoor bickering. The King Of The Eagles wanted to see what new, annoying outrage the goblins were up to now.

A very good thing, too! Terrible things were going on down there. It was high summer and there had not been much rain. There were a lot of dried branches and dead leaves that had now caught fire. Pantsoff had inadvertently set fire to all the tinder at the base of the trees they had climbed. He had stopped the rargs' attack, but in their place was a circle of fire that would eventually burn the dwarves alive. The Company's only hope was that the smoke would kill them first. They were no longer applauding Pantsoff.

To make matters worse, the goblins had arrived. They were disappointed that the slaughter of the woodsmen and their families had been rescheduled, but they were delighted that the murderers of their beloved Gobfather had been caught.

The goblin captain approached the Rarg chief and they spoke.

"Hey *paisan*!" said the goblin, "I understand you guys caught the rats what whacked our Gobfather."

"Rrrrr" said the rarg.

73

"This place is a mess," said the goblin. "What caught fire first?"

"Bark," said the rarg.

"Oh yeah," said the goblin. "So how's your night been?"

"Rough," said the rarg.

"I'll bet," said the goblin. "Where are the prisoners?"

"Roof," said the rarg.

"Of course!" said the goblin, looking up. "I see them. Thanks buddy. We'll take it from here."

The goblins figured the fire set by Pantsoff would soon do their work for them, so they sat down around the fire and taunted the doomed company.

Fifteen birds in five fir trees
K-I-S-S-I-N-G
First comes love
Then comes marriage
Then comes Bulbo in a baby carriage

"Hey Borin!" shouted one of the goblin *capos*. "Come on down! I wanna make you an offer you can't refuse!"

"Oh yeah?" shouted Pantsoff in answer. Smoke was in his eyes and throat, and it was getting very hot, so that was the best he could do under the circumstances. The goblins started a new song:

Dwarves, Dwarves, go away
Come again some other day
Or stay there up in those trees
You'll all be dead by morning

Burn, burn, beards will blaze
Fat will melt and eyes will glaze
Skin will crack and bones will black
You'll all be dead by morning

And with that, the flames were under Pantsoff's tree. Then it spread to the other trees. The bark caught fire, and the lower branches crackled.

Pantsoff climbed to the top of the tree. Magic flashed from the top of his wand like revolving blue lightning. He got ready to spring from on high right down into the goblins, magnificently killing himself, and possibly a few of them too.

"Is this the end of Pantsoff?" he cried, to no one in particular. But then, as was often the case in Pantsoff's plans, the unexpected happened. Just at that moment, as Pantsoff was about to immolate the goblins, the King Of The Eagles swept down from above, seized Pantsoff in his talons, and was gone.

There was a howl of anger and surprise from Pantsoff. It really hurts to be seized in an eagle's talons, whatever their intentions. The goblins were angry and surprised too.

The rargs howled their terrible "Rut-ros!" as they saw other eagles seizing the dwarves in their talons. Somehow, despite their eagle eyes that saw Pantsoff's fireworks from miles away, the eagles missed Bulbo and almost left him behind.

As the last eagle seized Tori, Bulbo grabbed at him. His well-marbled and surprisingly strong hands gripped Tori's ankles like a shoe salesman on commission.

The tree burst into flames below them, and Tori kicked at Bulbo saying "My legs! My poor legs!" to which Bulbo replied "My back! My poor back!"

As the large and amazingly strong eagle soared higher and higher with his two passengers, Bulbo, partly by accident, glanced down. His view of the burning trees and rargs, now far below him, was too much for him. He started to climb up Tori's legs. His goal, if he could have articulated it, was to either crawl into Tori's steel cable-knit sweater, or to weave himself into Tori's beard. Tori was kicking furiously, his goal being to help the eagle get rid of any excess weight, specifically Bulbo.

Before either of them could succeed, the eagle breathed a huge sigh of relief and dropped them both onto the rough platform of his eyrie. They lay still for a moment, enjoying the sensation of being alive. Then they sat up and silently tried not to look at each other, embarrassed by their behavior during the rescue flight.

"So, this is an eyrie!" said Bulbo, attempting to break the silence. "Until now, I've only ever used that word in crossword puzzles!"

"Um, yeah," said Tori. "Is an eyrie the same as an aerie?"

The eagle circled back and landed next to them. This eagle was absolutely huge, of course, huge enough to carry a dwarf and a wobbit. Huge enough to consider either of them as a meal. He looked at them for moment. Bulbo and Tori said nothing.

"Don't worry," the eagle said, "We're under strict orders from the King Of The Eagles to rescue you unharmed. I'm just the Sergeant At Arms Of The Eagles, so I do as I'm told."

Another eagle flew up. "The Chef Of The Eagles bids us to bring the prisoners to the Great Shelf for dinner," he said. "I'll carry the little one, you carry the one with the Fu Manchu beard."

The eagles carried their now-terrified passengers to the Great Shelf, which, despite its greatness, was far too narrow to please Bulbo. There he saw Pantsoff talking with the King Of The Eagles.

"Oh no!" thought Bulbo. "He's trying to talk them out of eating us! He's just going to make them angry!" Then he heard what Pantsoff was saying.

"—yes, tell your chef that rabbit and lamb will be perfect, thank you. And if you can have them bring up some firewood, we'll cook it ourselves. I know you prefer yours raw."

"Suit yourself, Pantsoff," said the King Of The Eagles. "And thanks again for taking that arrow out of my leg all those years ago. I trust we're even now," he said, waiting for Pantsoff to start negotiating.

"Yes, yes, of course! Thanks again!" said Pantsoff. Surprised but pleased, the King Of The Eagles flew off.

"Unbelievable," said Bulbo. "Do you know everyone?"

"Yes, I do," said Pantsoff. "And I'm glad the King Of The Eagles never found out it was my arrow that I pulled out of him. I shot it quite by accident, of course."

They talked with Borin and the others about their relief at being brought to the Great Shelf as dinner guests, and not as dinner entrées. The meat and firewood arrived. As they roasted their greasy tidbits, an eagle asked Pantsoff what time he'd like his wake-up call, and where he'd like to be flown after his complimentary breakfast.

Finally, they all ate their first meal since being imprisoned in the Moisty Mountains. After stuffing themselves with bloody, undercooked shreds of meat, they all slept for the first time since then, too. Bulbo slept more soundly than he ever had, even back at his apartment. But all night he dreamed he was back at school, taking an exam. Naked.

Chapter 7

QUEER LODGINGS FOR THE STRAIGHT WOBBIT

The next morning, Bulbo woke late, jumped up, and was about to move his pony cart to the other side of the street to avoid getting a parking ticket. Just before he stepped off the curb, he realized that he was on a mountain ledge.

Almost falling to his death would be the most terrifying thing to happen to Bulbo on a normal day. But on that particular day, the next thing he had to do was climb onto an eagle's back and be flown from the Great Shelf down to the Great Rock, which was far below them.

Bulbo clung desperately to the eagle, wishing that he had Tori to cling to instead. Tori had clothes to grip instead of slippery feathers, and he was unlikely to eat Bulbo for any reason.

"Nice morning." said the eagle in an attempt at small talk. "What is finer than flying?"

Bulbo opened his eyes but wisely chose not to answer. He inadvertently looked down, and then the almost-raw possum he had for breakfast started to come back up. He quickly closed his eyes and took deep breaths. Bulbo was pretty sure that eagles don't like it when you vomit on them.

"Next stop: The Great Rock," the eagle said, and landed with a bump. Bulbo opened his eyes again and climbed down, after making sure he hadn't forgotten any of his personal belongings.

"Bye bye now. Thanks for flying with us," said the eagle. That is the polite thing to say among eagles.

"Don't let your eyrie hit you on the way out," muttered Bulbo, which is not the correct reply. Fortunately, eagle ears aren't as sharp as eagle eyes.

And so they parted. And though the King Of The Eagles was later voted Bird Of The Year, Bulbo never saw him again—except in the Battle Of Six Or Seven Armies. But that comes in at the end of this tale. Please don't read ahead.

Below the Great Rock was a path and some steps leading down to a little cave. Borin told Wheeli and Deali to watch as Beefi and Bufu inspected the cave, to see how it's supposed to be done. All four of them declared the cave "100% Goblin-Free" and everyone entered, albeit cautiously.

Borin called the meeting of the day to order, and needlessly introduced Pantsoff as their guest speaker.

"Thank you, Borin," he began. "Overall, the adventure has gone extremely well. No one has been injured, lost or killed, and we've crossed the mountains, just as I planned. But now it's time for me to leave you."

He paused. "That's right. I'm leaving Borin & Company to follow up on some other projects."

There was absolutely no reaction from the dwarves or Bulbo.

"I know you're disappointed, but please hold back your objections, pleadings, bribes and tears, so you can hear me out."

Still, no reaction.

"Things haven't gone perfectly, I admit. There have been some hiccups along the way. The bad news is we have no ponies to carry our baggage. The good news is we have no baggage. No food, no tools or supplies, and no weapons of any sort besides my sword and Borin's. The even-better news is I know exactly where we are, and I know a guy who I guarantee will help us out. This guy is the person that cut the steps into this Great Rock. His 'Big Rock,' he calls it. Pretty impressive, huh?"

At the mention of someone who could be of more help than Pantsoff, the group became interested. They begged him to tell them who would help them and how, but all he would say was "I'll tell you when we get there."

They rested for a bit and wished they had some lunch. They then left the Great Rock and marched through some Great Grass, and later, some Great Trees.

Bulbo wasn't anxious to strike up a conversation with Pantsoff, especially now that he was planning to leave their group. But Bulbo was curious, as were the others, about what was to happen next.

"Hey, Pantsoff!" he said, "That was a great presentation you made this morning."

"Thanks," was all Pantsoff said. He was uncharacteristically quiet.

"He calls it 'Big Rock' instead of "Great Rock?'"

"I have no idea why. That's just what he calls it.

"Who is this 'He?' A king or something? "

"No, he's just a really great guy."

"Nice? Helpful? Famous?"

"No. Great as in huge. Physically huge. I'm pretty sure he'll help us."

"Pretty sure? You guaranteed his help before."

"That may have been an overstatement. Anyway, we have to be careful when we ask for his help. He gets angry easily, and he's very dangerous when he's angry. Or when he's sad. Or when he's excited, confused or happy. The important thing is that we not annoy him."

Upon hearing this, the dwarves crowded around and started asking questions again. "Is this the guy you're taking us to? Couldn't you take us to someone more even-tempered? Hadn't you better explain it all a bit more clearly?"

"Your answers," said Pantsoff, "are yes, no, and no, in that order. But since you ask, his name is Bjork, and he is a skin-changer."

"A what?" said Rori. "You mean a man that traps animals and changes their skins into coats, rugs and stoles?"

"Great Elephants, no! And while we're within a hundred furlongs of his home, don't mention stoles, skins or muffs of beaver, fox, vixen, cougar or bunny!"

Everyone gave Pantsoff a look.

"Because he loves animals, and they love him!" said Pantsoff.

"Ohhh!" said everybody else.

"They work for him," said Pantsoff, "and talk to him, and he protects and cares for them. He loves all animals. Except the evil ones, like rargs, bats, and giant spiders."

"Giant what?" said Bulbo. "What are you talking about?"

"He's a vegetarian, of course," said Pantsoff, ignoring Bulbo's question, "although he eats honey and cream, and possibly eggs. Maybe fish, too. I'm not sure."

"You said he was a skin-changer?" said Bulbo.

"Yes, I was getting to that. Sometimes he is a great strong man, and sometimes he is a huge, ferocious swan!"

"Really?" said Fallin. "A giant swan? How dangerous could a swan be?"

"Let's hope we don't find out," said Pantsoff. He kept them walking until, at mid-afternoon, they walked past a great many beehives. After that, they passed through vast gardens. The vegetables and fruits themselves were immense. Each kidney bean was bigger than your thumb. Bulbo had never seen anything like them.

"If I should eat a bowl of those," he said, "I should swell up as big again as I am!"

"Yes," said Pantsoff, "Bjork is famous for his vegetarian chili. He uses it in trade with the woodsmen and lumberjacks. Quiet, now, we're getting near his place."

They stood outside the gate to Bjork's compound. There were more gardens and a cluster of low wooden buildings inside. The buildings were made of unshaped logs, like vacation homes in Wisconsin.

"I'm going to lead the way, of course," said Pantsoff. "Bulbo, you'd better come with me. The rest of you, come in twos when I whistle. If you do exactly as I say there's a chance he'll help us."

"You were pretty sure of his help a minute ago," said Borin.

"Let's not waste time!" said Pantsoff. "Come on, Bulbo!"

As they entered the gate, two horses approached them and spoke. "Weh-heh-heh-heh-heh-helcome!" one horse said. "Wait he-he-he-he-here."

Bulbo whispered to Pantsoff "Bjork's horses are amazing and irritating at the same time!"

"Wait until you meet his goats!" said Pantsoff quietly.

A great, big man walked up. He was huge, as Pantsoff said he would be. He was shirtless and barefoot, wearing only some tattered purple pants.

Bulbo whispered, "You didn't mention that his skin is bright green!"

"What you want with Bjork?" the man asked.

"I am Pantsoff," said the wizard.

"Okay," said Bjork. "Who him?"

"That is Mr. Bunkins, a wobbit," said Pantsoff. Bulbo bowed. "And I am a wizard and project manager. I believe you know my cousin Everlast The Brown, who lives near the edge of Murkywood."

"Yes, is good wizard. What you want?" Bjork said again, more forcefully.

"To tell you the truth," said Pantsoff, "we've lost our way and our luggage and we need some advice. I may say that we had rather a bad time with some goblins in the mountains."

"Goblins bad! Bjork hate goblins! Goblins make Bjork mad!"

"Yes, of course," said Pantsoff in calm, even tones. "We don't like them either. They surprised us at night. There we were—do you have a minute? This is a long tale."

"Bjork has minute. Come sit in parlor," he said, and he brought them into the main building.

They followed him into a large, sparsely decorated room. They sat on some low, sturdy-looking furniture. There was a fire in the fireplace, and a view of a lovely flower garden through the window.

"Bjork like pansies! Pansies good!"

"Yes, and we do too, right, Bulbo?" said the wizard. "So as I was saying, I was coming over the mountains with a friend or two—"

"Where other friend?"

So Pantsoff whistled away and presently Borin and Tori came round the house by the garden path.

"This is Borin Oakmanfield and Tori," said Pantsoff, "and this is the incredible Bjork."

The dwarves both completed the introduction with the words "At your service."

"Oakmanfield?" said Bjork. "Service? Poor customer service from bank make Bjork mad! Bjork no need SmithiBank! Bjork prefer subsistence farming and barter."

"Yes," interrupted Pantsoff, before Borin could object. "You'll be pleased to know the new SmithiBank is committed to an improved customer experience. Right, Borin?"

"Yes, yes," said Borin. "The customer's always right, and so forth."

Pantsoff went on. "Like I was saying, Borin and Tori were on their way to visit family away east beyond Murkywood. There I was! We were crossing the Moisty Mountains and there was a terrible storm. Two giants were playing troll-dodgeball, and we hid in a cave, the wobbit and I and several of our companions—"

"Two dwarves not several."

"Exactly, Bjork, you're right," said Pantsoff. He whistled. "There's more. They'll be here in a minute. They didn't want to come in right away. They're bashful and sleepy."

"Traditional dwarf names. Good!"

"Actually, their names are Rori and Gori. Here they are now!" Introductions were made, and Pantsoff continued.

"While we were asleep, goblins entered through a secret door and captured us. We were taken—"

"Who on watch duty? Sleeping on watch make Bjork mad!"

"Right again, Bjork!" Pantsoff said, interrupting, but trying to stay calm and polite. He whistled. "But what's done is done, and assigning blame, if that's even possible in this case, isn't important. Oh look, more dwarves! Fallin and Crawlin, come meet the incredible Bjork!"

"Dwarves keep coming."

"Yes, they do! So there we were, in the cave. I managed to transform a few goblins into kettle-corn—"

"Kettle-corn make Bjork mad! Bjork prefer Extra-Butter!"

"Right! No kettle-corn!" Pantsoff whistled. "So the dwarves and their ponies appeared before the Gobfather—"

"Ponies? Ponies good. Bjork like ponies! Where ponies now?"

"Don't tell him!" whispered Bulbo desperately. "Lie! Say anything!"

"Um, well," said Pantsoff, who quickly whistled. "We're not sure." There was an awkward silence.

"You eat ponies?" said Bjork pointedly.

"Goodness no! The goblins ate them. You see--"

"Nooo!" Tears streamed down Bjork's mighty face. "Goblins bad. Bjork hate goblins! Bjork smash!"

"Wait Bjork, look!" said Pantsoff, desperate for an interruption. "Look, more dwarves!" In came Wheeli and Deali.

"Look Bjork! Singing dwarves!" Pantsoff then spoke quickly and with deadly seriousness to the dwarves. "Sing the 'Chip The Glasses' number! Sing!"

The dwarves began singing, and they improvised a mincing little dance number to go with it.

"Look Bjork, look! Bjork like singing dwarves!" said Pantsoff, and for once he was right. The song and dance routine was delightful, and Bjork quickly calmed down. Pantsoff whistled again.

""Dwarves good!" said Bjork with a smile on his broad, green face. He clapped along and laughed. The reprise was a success, especially the "Ho, Heigh-Ho, Heigh-Ho" part, where Bjork joined in, along with Pantsoff and Bulbo.

Loin and Groin entered, and Pantsoff gestured to them to join in on the last verse. Their introductions could wait. Beefi, Bufu and Fatso entered during the encore, where Fatso stole the show with some comedy ballet steps. Eventually, Bjork's laughter died down.

"Good times with little friends," he said. "Who hungry?"

Inside the living room it was now quite dark. Bjork took the company to a huge dining room, featuring more sleek but sturdy furniture. They all sat at a blonde-wood table.

"Bjork hungry!" he said loudly. An owl flew in. "Bjork has guests!"

"Who?" said the owl.

"Thirteen dwarves, one wizard, one wobbit," said Bjork. "Bring booster seat for wobbit, and one Kid's Menu."

"That's all right Bjork," said Pantsoff. "Bulbo's fully grown and he'll eat anything. No kidding."

"Bjork apologize. Everybody different." Some raccoons quickly set the table for sixteen. Two deer entered with mead in flagons. Once they poured the wine, Bjork proposed a toast.

"Differences good! Goblins bad!"

Everyone echoed the toast and drank. Sparrows flew in with napkins, and tied them around everyone's necks. This made Bulbo think they might be having barbecued ribs, but then he remembered Bjork's alternative vegetarian lifestyle. He then hoped for lobster, until a dozen squirrels dragged in bread, honey and butter, and a skunk entered with some cheese. The service seemed somehow unsanitary to Bulbo, and he was disappointed that a continental breakfast was served to him as a dinner, but he kept quiet and tried to have a nice time.

As mice cleared the table, Bjork spoke of Murkywood Forest. He discussed Murkywood's various points of interest, identifying each of them as either good or bad. They were mostly bad. Fortunately, a full stomach seemed to keep him from getting upset.

The dwarves all voiced their concerns about Murkywood. They weren't looking forward to marching through such a "bad" place. The deer came back with hot towels, and as everybody wiped their faces and hands, a possum and her young served coffee. A badger offered brandy, which Bjork declined. The dwarves were now discussing banking, and he was becoming drowsy.

"Busy day for Bjork. Good night," he said, and then went off to bed. The talk of compound interest and fee-based services was making Bulbo sleepy, too. He was soon dozing, but awoke to hear the dwarves singing.

They had been drinking for hours by that time, and were now quite morose. With voices full of nostalgia, longing and regret, their song put Bulbo right back to sleep:

> *Should old acquaintance be forgot*
> *And never brought to mind*
> *We'll close down SmithiBank for good*
> *Then we'll open up a mine*
>
> *The dragon, we could all ignore*
> *Only Mountain, leave behind*
> *We'd dig for gold like dwarves before*
> *And for jewels in our mine*
>
> *Let's dig gold in our mine, my dears*
> *Let's dig gold in our mine*
> *We'll drink from cups of platinum*
> *That we dug out of our mine*

Later, when everyone was asleep, Bulbo's back hurt so much it woke him up. Sleeping in a booster seat had been a mistake. As he was looking for a comfortable place to stretch out with proper back support, he thought he heard something.

There was a honking sound outside, and the noise of some great animal pecking at the door. Bulbo wondered what it was, and whether it could be Bjork in enchanted shape, and if he would come in as a giant swan and kill them. Bulbo dived under Crawlin's ZZ Top beard and hid his head. There he fell asleep at last, in spite of his fears.

It was full morning when Bulbo awoke. Breakfast was provided, and was exactly the same as their dinner the night before. As Bulbo ate with the dwarves, attended by Bjork's woodland busboys, he noticed how quiet the room was. Then he noticed something else.

"Where's Pantsoff?" Bulbo asked. Nobody knew, and as long as the mead, bread, butter and honey kept coming, they didn't care.

Bjork wasn't around either. He seemed nice enough, but it was a relief that he was gone. They found it exhausting trying to not make him mad. The drinking and eating continued through lunch until dinner, when Pantsoff finally showed up.

"Good evening, all!" he said, grandly. No one said anything in return.

"Please, please, hold your questions until after supper! I haven't eaten since breakfast." Bulbo didn't know if that meant breakfast served in the morning, or the breakfast at noon, but he wasn't about to ask. Neither were the dwarves. Pantsoff ate what must have been two meals at least to make up for missing his lunch.

"I'm sure you're all curious about where I've been all day," he said. "I've been picking out swan-tracks. There must have been a regular swan's convention just outside last night. Bjork couldn't have made all those tracks himself. The largest ones eventually went straight to the Big Rock. I followed them that far. From there they headed straight to the rargs' meeting place in the woods. That's where, you may remember, we were recently rescued from the rargs and goblins, thanks to me and my vast network of Little Earth's Power Elite.

"Yes," said Borin. "Thanks for the reminder of a dreadful event from all of two days ago. Yes, we all remember."

"What shall we do!" said Bulbo. "Bjork went to a meeting with the rargs? And probably the goblins, too! He'll lead them back here!"

"Bulbo, please stop it," said Fallin. "Surely you remember Bjork's eloquent statement on his relationship with the goblins. 'Bjork hate goblins! Bjork smash!' is what he said, I think."

"Oh, that's right," said Bulbo. "I guess that's the mead talking. I better go to bed."

The dwarves started singing again, so Bulbo was asleep in no time. He dreamed he had caught a swan, and was eating it. He woke up with feathers in his mouth and his pillow was gone. Bulbo went through a lot of pillows. As he fell back asleep he heard honking and pecking, as he did the night before.

Next morning they were wakened by the incredible Bjork himself. The only thing more startling than seeing Bjork's gigantic green face is seeing it as soon as you wake up. Bjork was in a jolly mood, which made him almost as dangerous as when he was angry.

"Who hungry? Bjork like breakfast!" he said to Bulbo, and to each of the dwarves. They all headed to the breakfast table where Pantsoff was waiting.

"Good morning everyone. Have a seat," he said. There was a lot of sighing and eye-rolling. The dwarves all knew a Pantsoff Speech was coming.

"Bjork, our host, would like to say a few words," Pantsoff said. The dwarves were glad Pantsoff was only the emcee. On the other hand, they hoped Bjork would have no upsetting things to discuss. Those nearest him discretely backed away, just in case.

"Bjork visit Rarg glade. Bjork see ashes. Wizard tell truth. Truth good!" The dwarves applauded politely.

"Bjork catch goblin and rarg. Goblin tell Bjork everything."

"Did he torture them?" Bulbo whispered to Pantsoff. The thought of anyone being tortured by Bjork was a terrifying one. Bjork glanced up at Bulbo.

"Bjork no use torture. Torture bad!"

The dwarves prepared a quick song-and-dance to keep Bulbo from getting smashed, but Bjork continued his presentation.

"Goblin say wizard smash Gobfather. Wizard good!" Pantsoff bowed slightly. "So Bjork help wizard and little friends.

"Bjork advise little friends three things. Number One: in Murkywood, don't leave path! Bjork give friends everything they need to get through: food, blankets, bows and arrows—"

"For hunting?" asked Rori.

Borin kicked him under the table with a massive, iron-bound wingtip, and whispered "Not in front of the waiters!" who were mostly deer.

"Number Two: in forest, no drink river water! Murkywood water bad! Bjork give friends water to carry. Bjork also lend ponies for start of long journey.

"Number Three: Friends no take ponies into forest. Send ponies back! Forest bad!

"Have pleasant trip!" Bjork concluded, and went to run some errands.

Their spirits sank at his grave words. Even Rori and Tori were starting to realize how dangerous this trip was. Their one comfort was that they had Bulbo along to kill the dragon that was waiting for them at the end.

The next morning, after one last predictable breakfast, they packed the supplies Bjork loaned them and rode off through the gate.

Hung up next to the gate was what looked like a rarg skin. On closer examination, they saw that the skin still had the rarg in it, smashed flat. On the other side of the gate was a goblin in similar condition.

"I thought Bjork said he didn't torture his captives," said Bulbo.

"They show no signs of torture," said Pantsoff. Which was true enough.

"A swan did this, really?" said Fallin.

"Are you the only one here who never tried to catch a swan when you were a kid?" said Pantsoff. The other dwarves winced as they shared their childhood experiences of swans fighting back.

"Now imagine a swan ten feet tall, with Bjork's temper!" said Pantsoff. "Bjork is a fierce enemy. A dangerous friend, too. Let's go before he hears us and we have to dance again."

They rode on, stopping only to sleep or eat Bjork's famous "breakfast served all day" yet again. There was no sign of Bjork's Famous Veggie Chili, which would have been a wonderful change of pace. At night, Bulbo thought he saw the shadowy form of a huge swan prowling in the bushes. But if he dared to mention it to Pantsoff, the wizard only said "Hush! Act nonchalant!"

After four days of this, they reached the eaves of Murkywood. The trees were huge, gnarled and angry-looking.

"Well, here is Murkywood forest," said Pantsoff, "just as promised. You've all arrived safe and sound. Time to send your ponies back."

"What about your horse?" asked Borin.

"Never you mind. I'm not entering Murkywood, thank goodness. I have some pressing business away south. An All-Wizard Annual Golf Outing, with many important decisions to be made in a productive, informal setting. I have to leave first thing tomorrow if I want to get there in time for the Free Appetizers And Cocktails Kick-Off Mixer. So start unpacking those ponies!"

As soon as their packs were removed, the ponies ran directly away from the forest, faster than anyone had seen them run before.

"It's almost as if the forest frightened them, in some way," noted Beefi. Pantsoff nodded knowingly.

The next morning Pantsoff woke everyone early to give his goodbye address. In it, he recounted all his accomplishments during the trip, and invented several more.

"Goodbye!" he finally said. "And don't stray off the path!"

"Do we really have to go through this dreadful forest, Pantsoff?" Bulbo asked.

"Not at all," Pantsoff said. "You could go two hundred miles around to the north, or four hundred miles around to the south. Both paths are chock full of goblins, hobgoblins, and hemogoblins that are all dying to eat you. Not to mention the dark tower of the Neccomancer. I'm not going to discuss him further, because you would abandon your project in terror. I will only say this: going near him makes walking the path through Murkywood seem fairly conservative and well-reasoned.

"Stay on the path, hope for the best and expect the worst. With a tremendous slice of Luck Pie Ala Mode, you may come out one day. After all that, killing Smog will be like taking the day off. If you can employ the element of surprise, that is.

"Thanks for the pep-talk, Pantsoff," said Borin. "You were just leaving, right?"

"Yes, yes, of course," said Pantsoff. He could not resist the temptation to have the last word, as always, so he turned back as they entered the forest to yell "DON'T LEAVE THE PATH!"

They turned and looked back at him as he rode off.

Bulbo simply said "What a pest." In silent agreement, the dwarves shouldered their heavy packs and water skins. As they left the open air and entered the forest, their spirits sank like a wobbit in swimming class.

Chapter 8

GUYS VERSUS SPIDERS

They walked in a pitiful, single file. Over the entrance
to the forest was an arch with the sign: "Welcome to the
Murkywood Forest." Then in small letters below, "While in
Murkywood, please refrain from smoking, spitting, or playing
loud music."

"Oh man!" said Tori. "What's left? There's nothing to
do now except march through!"

In very small letters at the bottom of the sign were the
words "Warning! Do not march through Murkywood Forest.
The Murkywood Wood-Elf Lodge cannot be held liable for
your deaths. Thank you for your cooperation. –The
Murkywood Wood-Elf Lodge."

"Pantsoff said we should stay on the path," said Rori.
"So maybe we should look for a shortcut instead."

"I'd agree with you," said Borin, "based on Pantsoff's
advice so far. But Bjork said to stay on the path, so that's
what we're going to do. If not, he might find out from one of
his woodland friends that we ignored his advice. I don't want
him to get mad and come looking for us. 'Bjork smash!' and
so forth."

The path became dimmer and dimmer. It was like
being in a movie theatre, but without any light coming from
the screen, the exits, or anyone's phone. There was only a
darkened green glimmer that allowed the company to see a
little way into the trees on either side.

It was quieter than a movie theatre, too. There were no
cries of "Oh no he didn't!" or "Lookout girlfriend!" or
"We're over here, Ricky!" Instead, there were queer noises,

92

queer even to Bulbo's ears: snufflings, scurryings and toots in the undergrowth, made by unseen creatures. This, too, was like being in a movie theatre, depending on the type of movies you go to.

There were cobwebs everywhere, too, and worse than you'd see in your grandma's garage. No one stopped to wonder why the web-strands were extraordinarily thick. There were none stretched across the path, and the company soon found out why. Next to the path was a sign that read: "This path kept clear by the Murkywood Wood-Elf Lodge. Please don't litter."

It was not long before they grew to hate the forest as much as the tunnels of the goblins or the small talk of Pantsoff. They wished he was with them, not because they needed him or missed him, but because they wanted him to share their misery. By the time they stopped for lunch, they were all in deep despair over the dark, the stillness, and the stuffiness. It was like being in a bowling alley on a weekday afternoon.

At night, the forest went from being dark to being really dark. They had never seen anything like it, darker even than the goblin tunnels from which they had just recently escaped. They slept cuddled up like spoons, partially because of the ambient creepiness of Murkywood, and partially because old habits die hard.

Being on watch was the worst. Bulbo could see the gleam of eyes, lots of eyes. Eyes of all sizes. Some were huge bulbous eyes, like you might see on a giant insect. "Thank goodness for all those giant spider webs," Bulbo thought.

They tried lighting watch fires at night, but they soon gave up. The fires drew thousands of moths, which in turn brought bats. The bats were huge and as black as top hats, with teeth as white as a new pair of spats.

Days followed days. The forest never changed, much like the food Bjork packed for them. They decided Bjork's absent chili must be for official use only, never eaten by Bjork or his friends. Bulbo was always hungry, because Borin was cheap, and very careful with the provisions. They tried shooting at the black squirrels that scurried around in the trees, and finally brought one down on the path after losing

93

many arrows. They roasted it for dinner, but it was horrible to taste, and the portions were too small.

They were running low on water, too, and the forest offered none of that, either. When they found their first stream, it was blocking their path. Its current was as strong and black as convenience-store espresso. Bulbo was so thirsty he was willing to drink from it, perhaps with steamed milk and hazelnut syrup. But Bjork said not to, so he didn't.

They didn't even want to touch the water after his warning of "water bad." But there was no bridge, and they had to cross it.

"Where are those wood-elves when you need them?" Borin said. "They say that they maintain this path! Couldn't they put a bridge up?"

"Wait a minute!" said Bulbo. He was peering across the river, hoping to see a drinking fountain or café. "I see a boat against the far bank!"

"Excellent!" said Borin. "Be a good lad and go get it. You can probably just wade across."

Bulbo silently disagreed. He grabbed a huge black moth that had been fluttering around his head and threw it into the water. As soon as it hit the water, it stopped moving and floated quickly downstream.

"I'm not sure what your demonstration is supposed to prove," said Borin, "but perhaps one of us could throw a rope to the boat and pull it over? Mr. Bunkins, I assume you can't throw that far. Gori, you used to play quarterback for the old SmithiBank rootball team, but Deali, you have the best eyesight."

"Everyone knows that I have the best eyesight here!" said Fallin.

"Everyone thought you had the best eyesight," said Deali, "until Bulbo got past you on guard duty. You're out, see? And Gori, you threw mostly interceptions. I'm throwing the rope!"

With that, Deali took the rope and one of the grappling hooks Bjork had provided, and started throwing. His first few tosses missed, much to Fallin and Gori's delight. Soon, though, one of his throws caught the boat and he pulled it to them.

"Good work!" said Borin. "And now, Bulbo, you just row across. Make sure the boat is sound and the other side of the river is safe. We'll wait here."

Bulbo got in the boat and looked at the decades' worth of dead leaves, live insects, and mold inside it. "At least it's not leaking."

He rowed across and looked nervously down the path. He called back to the dwarves through the dimness.

"I'm on the other side. There's no trolls, giants, goblins, or rargs. A lot of huge spider webs, but no signs of danger. Now what?"

"Well," Borin said, "Row back over!"

"You're the boss," said Bulbo, as he rowed back over to the dwarves.

"Excellent!" said Borin. "On this trip, I'll row over with you, Wheeli and Fallin. Let's go!"

They all got into the boat. Before the started rowing, Bulbo spoke up.

"I don't want to be pushy, but couldn't we tie the rope to the boat and have Fatso pull it back instead of having me row it back? That way we wouldn't lose a space in the boat each trip."

"So the traditional dwarf ways aren't good enough for our consultant?" said Borin. "Have it your way. Fatso, hold the rope!"

Bulbo rolled his eyes, tied the rope, and got back into the boat. They rowed across, and Fatso pulled it back. They were followed by Deali and Loin and Groin and Rori, and then Gori and Rori and Beefi and Bufu.

"So we're to be last," said Fatso to Crawlin. "I'm always last. Go ahead, pick on the fat guy."

"How is it you're still so fat even though we're on short rations?" asked Crawlin as he got into the boat.

"I don't know," said Fatso. "I've tried everything. It must be my metabolism."

As Fatso stepped one foot into the boat, a jet black bull moose ran down the path towards the river, straight at Fatso. Shocked, Fatso grabbed at his chest. The moose leapt over Fatso and the river, but landed with an arrow in its heart from Borin's bow. Borin was really hungry, and badly wanted meat instead of honey. The moose left the path and stumbled deep into the forest. The dwarves were about to stumble after it when Bulbo stopped them.

"Fatso has fallen in! Fatso is drowning!" cried Bulbo. Crawlin was so hungry that he had rowed all the way across without noticing that Fatso was missing from the boat. He grudgingly put all thoughts of fresh meat out of his head and rowed back to rescue Fatso.

Fatso was floating near the bank where he had suffered another angina attack, brought on by the startling appearance of the moose. There he flopped down senseless, unfortunately not into the boat, but into the espresso-like magic river instead. Crawlin struggled to avoid touching the water as he pulled the heavy, unconscious dwarf out of the swift current.

"Drag him into the boat!" the other dwarves cried from the far bank.

"Why don't *you* drag him into the boat!" Crawlin called back. "Do you have any idea how heavy this guy is?"

Crawlin managed to get Fatso partially into the boat, and then rowed to the other dwarves, who pulled the limp soggy Fatso onto the bank.

"Let's bury him and get moving," said Borin.

"But he's still alive," said Bulbo.

"What?"

"He's still breathing," said Bulbo. "He's just unconscious. It must be some sort of sleeping magic from the river. That's why Bjork told us not to drink its water." Bulbo was right: the river had a magic about it that put all who touched it into a deep sleep, in a way very much unlike espresso.

"Okay," said Borin. "Wake him up then."

"How?" said Crawlin. "Splash water in his face? We pulled him out of a river!"

"Why do I have to think of everything?" Borin kicked Fatso in his fleshy ribs a few times, but the dwarf didn't respond. He tried poking him with a stick.

"I still say we bury him," he said.

"Borin, he's not dead!" said Bulbo.

"Then let's leave him here until he wakes up," said Borin. "He'll be fully refreshed and able to catch up with us on his own. He can move pretty quick for a big guy."

"I can't believe this!" said Bulbo, who had been treated kindly by Fatso in the past. "We've got to take him with us. We'll take turns dragging him."

And drag him they did, a difficult task made even worse by the dopey smile on Fatso's sleeping face. They had never seen him so happy.

They dragged Fatso for days, at first by his feet until Bulbo complained, and then by his collar. The good news was that with Fatso asleep all the time, the food consumption dropped considerably. But there was very little left all the same.

The forest remained dim and thick, much like Tori and Rori. The only change of pace was a mysterious laughing and singing they heard in the distance. Since the dwarves weren't being attacked, they figured the singing wasn't from goblins. They listened hard, but couldn't catch any of the lyrics.

After a few more days of endless marching, they ate the last of their bread and honey. There was some talk of eating Fatso, but when they put it to a vote, the decision was to save him for later. Then Fatso woke up, to the relief of some and the hungry disappointment of others.

"Where's all the food?" he said as he sat up, rubbing his eyes. "I dreamed I was at an elvish buffet and open bar."

"The food's all gone," said Borin.

"No food at all?" said Fatso. "But I'm starving!"

"We're all starving, Fatso. Literally. If we keep marching, some of us may make it out of this forest alive. Nourished, if necessary, by whoever dies first. And by the way, you're welcome. We've spent the last week dragging you as you slept. Now march!"

At that very moment, Fallin, who was a little way ahead, called out "Hey! I saw a twinkle of light in the forest!"

"I saw it first!" said Deali.

They all looked and soon saw dozens of torchlights in the distant trees, a good way off the path.

"My dream has come true!" said Fatso. "Bonfires! Buffet! Open bar! Me first!" He ran off into the forest.

"Hooray!" yelled the others. They followed, without even a moment's reflection on the warnings from Bjork.

Bulbo was deeply concerned about how things were likely to turn out, but did not want to be left behind alone, so he ran with the others.

They all approached a clearing that had been nicely decorated with tiki torches, balloons and streamers. There, enjoying a cheerful cookout, were elves. Elves singing, elves cooking ribs, elves eating pretzels, elves playing horseshoes, elves drinking beer. The smell of barbecue was too much for the dwarves, and they burst into the clearing.

With that, the tiki torches, bonfire and barbecue grills all went out, extinguished as if by magic. The lawn chairs, badminton nets, and hot dogs all vanished, and so did the elves.

It instantly became so completely dark that Bulbo could not find any of the dwarves. Even the Buddy System failed them. Everyone had run off following the sound of everyone else's voice. Bulbo was left all alone.

That was one of his most miserable moments of the adventure. There were many to choose from, and Bulbo was not even halfway through it. He decided to try to sleep until dawn, when it would be light enough to see a little.

He was dreaming of pouring a little extra cream into his coffee when he felt something touch his wrist. He woke and saw that it wasn't Fatso. It was a strong, sticky string. He tried to get up, but he discovered that his feet were wrapped in the same stuff. It was like the giant spider webs that they'd seen throughout Murkywood.

Finally, Bulbo understood. This silk was spun by a giant spider that wasn't trying to catch a fly—she was trying to catch Bulbo!

He turned, and there she was! A great, ugly spider! To his horror, she spoke to him.

"Salutations!" she said in a warm, gentle, feminine voice.

"Salu-*what?*" said Bulbo, a little confused as well as terrified.

"Salutations!" she said again. "That's just my fancy way of saying hello."

"What are you doing?"

"I'm wrapping you in silk so you can't move. Then I'm going to poison you with my bite. That way it won't hurt you so much when I suck out all your blood!"

"You're going to kill me?"

"I'm afraid so. I'm not entirely happy about my diet, but that's the way I'm made. So it's been with my mother and all her mothers before her, all the way back long ago to the quiet of the world. Now, try to make yourself comfortable while I—"

Bulbo appreciated the spider's gentle, reassuring manner, but he really didn't want to be eaten. He flailed furiously with his arms in true Dork fashion as she tried to finish her job of wrapping him.

Then he had a sensation of mental clarity unlike any he had ever known. He knew at that moment that his only hope was to quickly kill this monster with his knife. He felt capable of defending himself, and he felt no need to shriek like a little girl.

"Stop wiggling!" said the spider. Her scolding gave Bulbo a moment to reach his Elf Army Knife. He tried to open the main blade, but got the combination bottle opener/screwdriver instead. Like the can opener, it was really dirty and stinky.

"Just what do you think you're doing?" she asked. He closed the bottle opener, quickly tried for another tool and was able to open the main blade before the spider realized what was happening. She had never fought prey that carried a pocket knife.

Bulbo held the blade forward and the spider stepped back. "Let's not do anything we might regret. This may have been a simple misunderstanding!" she said brightly as she considered what to do next.

Bulbo took the opportunity to cut his legs free. Bulbo thought she looked surprised at how easily he cut the web, but he may have been wrong. It's hard to read expressions on the face of a spider. So he didn't anticipate her sudden, snapping attack.

Cowering was no good, so he leapt forward and met the spider's attack with a bloodcurdling wobbit yell. He avoided her poisoned jaws and stabbed her in the eye, which he could see more clearly than the rest of her in the dark. Then he killed her with a second, deeper stab in one of the other seven eyes. Fortunately, she was not very tough for a spider of any size.

Bulbo rested from the uncommon exertion of killing a monster bug as he looked at the dead spider and the weapon he used to kill her. Somehow his killing of the giant spider, without first begging for mercy or betraying his friends, made a great difference to Mr. Bunkins. He felt much fiercer and bolder in spite of his constant longing for a Quiche Lorraine and a hazelnut latte. Bulbo cleaned the blood off the main blade of his knife. It was the only blade that wasn't filthy and smelly, and he wanted to keep it that way.

"I shall give you a name," he said as he sniffed at it dubiously, "and I shall call you *Stink*."

Bulbo started planning. Normally, his plans would be only for his benefit and would not have included the dwarves except as bait or collateral. But he actually felt like he should try to help them if he could, or at least find them. He was concerned, for the first time ever, for their well-being. To be more accurate, he was concerned that he might feel guilty if he didn't help them, and Bulbo didn't want to have to deal with guilt on top of all his other problems.

He decided to start looking for the dwarves. This was an opportunity for him to trust his luck, the legendary "Luck Of The Dorkish." He had never felt lucky before, but he realized how amazingly lucky he had been to have survived the adventure this long. He put his finger in his magic ring, to give him a little more of an edge. Then he set off in search of the dwarves.

As he crept along, silent and invisible, he noticed the usual giant webs increasing in size and thickness. There seemed to be some irregularity in the web design, not the usual radiating straight lines with a spiral overlay. On closer inspection, Bulbo saw writing in the web. Neatly formed in block letters was a message. It said:

SOME DWARF!

"Now what?" Bulbo said to himself. "Borin and the others must be nearby." In the webs were more spiders, like the one he killed. Bulbo was ready to give up and turn back when he heard the spiders talking. They were talking about the dwarves!

"What do you think?" said one spider as she stepped back to admire the message. "All our sisters will know that we caught some dwarves! What a lovely change of pace from the usual elves and goblins!"

"Yes, very nice, dear," said another. "We can eat them for tea tomorrow! Everyone will be so pleased!"

"Perhaps we should wait a bit longer," said the first, in a sweet, thoughtful voice. "Let them hang a bit and tenderize. We can poison them again so they won't fuss."

"Let's not leave them hang for too long, though" said a third spider. "They don't appear to have been eating too well, the poor things. Except for the fat one." The spider ran to a branch with a dozen bundles of web hanging below it. Through the web, Bulbo could see bits of beard sticking out. Above the fattest bundle was another web, and neatly woven in block letters was the word:

TERRIFIC

Fatso was obviously their favorite.

The spider looked closely at a dwarfish nose sticking out of the largest bundle. To everyone's surprise, the bundle suddenly kicked, and knocked the spider down to a lower branch. She came back up in a hurry.

"Gracious!" she said to the bundle. "What are you doing up?"

Bulbo saw that the moment had come when he must do something. Unfortunately, his entire plan so far had been to look for the dwarves. There was no next step. He was at a loss, and wished he hadn't been so critical of Pantsoff's planning.

He knew he couldn't get to the dwarves quickly enough to save whoever was about to be poisoned. The spiders were all out of reach and couldn't be fought hand-to-hand. Bulbo had been looking forward to using his magic Elf Army Knife while invisible to really wreak some havoc, but it was not to be.

He could throw something at the spiders, of course. Actually, Bulbo was pretty good at throwing things, which was as close as any of the Dorks ever came to having athletic talent. Bulbo had always done well at games that involved throwing at targets, especially while drinking: bocce, jarts, horseshoes, cards in a hat, that sort of thing. He got more exercise from these games than anything else except eating lobster.

Bulbo quickly found a stone. Fortunately, the spider's lair was located over a gravel pit. He threw his stone at the spider that was about to poison Fatso, hoping to distract her. Incredibly, it hit the spider on the head. Even more incredibly, his one stone killed the giant spider! Bulbo was amazed that anything so large and scary could be killed so easily. He'd had more trouble killing the regular-size spiders that he found back in his Wobbiton apartment.

Thus encouraged, Bulbo kept throwing stones. Soon there were many dead spiders, and many more angry ones. It would be impossible to kill all of them before one of them was able to trap Bulbo in a web. Or they might decide to kill the dwarves right away, out of spite.

So Bulbo decided to lead them away from the dwarves. There was no way Bulbo was taking off his magic ring, so the spiders couldn't see him, but they knew in general where the thrown rocks were coming from. Just to be sure that they would follow him, Bulbo decided to taunt them with a song:

Two fat spiders sitting in a tree
K-I-S-S-I-N-G
First comes love
Then comes marriage
Then an egg-sack and a baby carriage

Old Tomnoddy sitting in a tree
Old Tomnoddy can't catch me!
At-ter-cop!
At-ter-cop!
Hey you spiders follow me!

Not very good, perhaps, and mostly stolen from the goblins, but Bulbo was in a bit of a rush. And it worked. The spiders followed him, partly out of anger, and partly to ask Bulbo what "Tomnoddy" and "Attercop" meant.

The spiders, about fifty of them, were trying to corner the invisible Bulbo by spinning web all around him. He had been expecting that, and was able to slip away as surely and silently as he might escape from a work-friend's retirement party.

He had to draw the spiders even further away from the dwarves before he began Part Two of his plan, which he had just thought up. There were no spiders within rock-throwing range, so he thought another song would be good. There was one song Bulbo knew that would infuriate any spider:

The itsy-bitsy spider
Went up to catch a fly
It never met
An insect such as I
Out came my knife
I stabbed it twice and then
The itsy-bitsy spider
Could not get up again

The great big spiders
Went up into the trees
Too old and fat to
Catch a guy like me
Out come the dwarves
I'll cut them loose and then
The bloated, dumbass spiders
Run up the trees again

Bulbo was especially proud that he could improvise so many elements of his fight into the song. And he felt that "dumbass" might be more to the point than "Tomnoddy" or "Attercop."

He soon discovered it was. Spiders were everywhere, and more coming. He still couldn't read their expressions very well, but their body language told Bulbo that these spiders were furious. So furious that they were making mistakes in their pursuit.

Web strands were flying everywhere, but the angry spiders had all assumed that someone else would complete the work, spinning proper webs to catch their invisible tormentor. A proper web might have gone a long way towards catching Bulbo. But as is so often the case during emotional times, many critical tasks were forgotten.

Bulbo was able to easily cut through the random, individual web strands using his knife's Pliers & Wire Cutter tool. If Bulbo had been carrying the "Steward" Elf Army Knife he could have used its special Web-Cutter blade, but Bulbo had only the "Thane" model. It had no web-cutter, and its toothpick, made of genuine Oliphaunt ivory, was long since lost.

The spiders' tactics were unimpressive. They were too upset to place a guard on the captive dwarves, despite the fact that Bulbo actually gave away his plan in his taunt song's second verse out of giddiness from bloodlust and songwriting.

As Bulbo ran back to Borin & Company, he was starting to realize that although his ring made him invisible, it didn't work on Stink. Rather, it didn't work on his weapon *while he was using it*. This was unfortunate, because being able to fight while completely invisible would have been handy in a tight spot.

He wished he had time for the extensive testing this matter required. Why was Stink invisible when folded and in his pocket? Would any type of weapon remain visible, or were there exceptions that he might discover? Perhaps weapons made of wood rather than metal? Could a billy club or a pointed stick be made invisible? What about his own body? If he used a fist or a foot to attack, would they become visible? Since his clothing remained invisible, could he develop weapons that were part of his clothing, like a razor-sharp bowtie or armor-piercing moccasins?

Any self-respecting Dork would happily spend hours figuring out the answers to Bulbo's questions, but now was not the time. He got hold of himself once he arrived at the dwarves' tree. He closed the Pliers & Wire Cutter and decided to try the Large Scissors. Thanks to some very low branches Bulbo climbed up the tree, and then out on the branch where the dwarves hung wrapped in web. There were no spiders anywhere nearby.

The Large Scissors worked perfectly. You can't do better than a magic elf-weapon. In just a few moments, Bulbo had cut all the bundles off the branch. Their fall was farther than Bulbo would have liked, but judging by the angry cries and violent thrashing, none of the dwarves were too badly hurt.

As he went to cut open the bundles, Bulbo removed his ring. The dwarves might still turn on him, even though he was rescuing them, so he wanted to keep his invisibility trick a secret to use later if necessary. In his visible state he reached for the first bundle.

"This is either Wheeli or Deali," he thought, looking at the bit of jazz beard sticking out of the bundle. Once Bulbo cut off the web-strands, Wheeli was slow to get up. He later described being a victim of spider-poison as "similar to being horribly hung over, without the benefit of getting drunk beforehand." He said nothing about the fall from the branch.

Encouraged by the threat of recapture by the spiders, Wheeli was able to help Bulbo unwrap the remaining dwarves. They were soon all up and about, although the spiders returned before Fatso could recover from his headache and nausea. Since he was the juiciest, the spiders attacked him first.

Thus the battle began: hundreds of angry giant spiders attacking Bulbo and a dozen woozy dwarves. Woozy, but awake and able to see, unlike the night before when they were captured. They were all able to arm themselves with big sticks, and there was an abundance of deadly rocks. The dwarves soon discovered how laughably vulnerable the spiders were, and merrily slaughtered them as they attacked. For a while the joy of battle revived them, but soon it started to wear them out. Bulbo was becoming exhausted, though his

105

knife shone brightly with elf magic as he killed spider after spider.

"Stink doesn't like spiders any more than it likes goblins," Bulbo thought as he stabbed another spider. His strength was almost used up, and the dwarves were just as tired. They were about to surrender and hope for another rescue. But suddenly the spiders gave up first and retreated. In the future they would avoid opponents that could fight using sticks and stones and name-calling. Attercop indeed!

The dwarves noticed they had fought their way back to the clearing where they had tried to crash the elf-cookout. The spiders were gone, so they all sat down to catch their breath. They had many concerns about finding food, water, and a way out of the forest, and they voiced these to Bulbo, as if he was their project manager.

They also were very curious about how Bulbo rescued them. Bulbo was so exhausted from the battle, the singing, and the improvisation of lyrics that he couldn't come up with a plausible lie. Against his better judgment, he told the truth in its entirety: the ring, Lady Gol-Gol, the riddle-game and the escape. Tori and Rori enjoyed the riddles so much they insisted on hearing that part of the story a second time, and they took turns shouting out the answers.

Knowing the truth about the Vanishing Mr. Bunkins did not lessen their opinion of Bulbo at all. In fact, dwarves in general have the greatest of respect for anyone who owns valuable objects like magic weapons and rings. They also place great value on good luck, and Bulbo was clearly very lucky. He was hired for the adventure so the dwarves could avoid setting out with an unlucky group of thirteen. Bulbo was thinking back to the day he became Borin's "lucky number" when he had a horrid realization.

"I cut down a dozen bundles," he said, "but there should be thirteen of you! Who's missing? Speak up!"

No one was barking out orders or making accusations, and soon it became clear who was missing. "Borin!" Bufu said.

They didn't know what to do. On the one hand they didn't like Borin or his banjo playing, and his departure would increase their share of the loot. True, he was related to most of them, but dwarves have large families and he would not be missed. There was one thing they could not overlook, though. Borin had the key! The key to the secret service entrance at One SmithiBank Plaza! Without Borin, or at least his key, Bulbo wouldn't be able to enter the corporate headquarters and kill the dragon.

They quickly gave Borin up for dead and assumed their adventure was over. They flopped down, giving up to sleep and, probably, death. Even Bulbo, the most positive and enthusiastic member of the group since Pantsoff left, was at a loss.

Borin was not dead, though. Not yet, at least, but he had been captured before any of the others. Not by spiders, fortunately, but by the elves that were trying to enjoy a cookout. He had actually asked one of the elves if they had any scotch whiskey just before the lights went out that first time. Then in the dark he was overpowered and carried away, along with the coolers, watermelons and volleyballs.

Wood-elves are not wicked, certainly not as wicked as goblins, or even as dwarves for that matter. They were quite different from the Hidden Valley elves. They tolerated but did not trust tourists. They preferred hunting, fishing, hockey and curling over cooking demonstrations, dance contests, sing-along concerts and wine-tastings. Predictably, wood-elves usually lived in the woods, often in lodges or cabins, rather than the resorts and hotels of the Hidden Valley. After the coming of Men (and Women), they withdrew and more and more took to living in cottages or even camps. Still, elves they are and remain, and that is Good People, if you can call beings that live for thousands of years "people."

In a great lodge some miles within the edge of Murkywood on the eastern side lived their greatest king. To this lodge they dragged Borin—not too gently either. In the old days, the Elvenking had lost a fortune in SmithiBank investments during a market adjustment, and he blamed it on the dwarves. It is only fair to say that the dwarves gave a different explanation and said that the investments were clearly identified as not being covered by deposit insurance. Thus they were subject to a loss in value. The Elvenking said he was seduced by promises of high returns on his money, but was actually very risk-averse. He felt he should have had his principal refunded to him as a show of good faith, which the dwarves never, ever do. The story was endlessly entertaining to the dwarves, and the topic of many of their songs. You will be relieved to know that I will not repeat any of those songs here.

Of course, Borin felt undeserving of the rough treatment he received. As he was being marched into the lodge, he vowed that no word of gold or jewels being recovered from SmithiBank's offices should ever be forced out of him.

In the throne room, the king looked sternly at Borin when he was brought before him. He asked Borin many difficult questions.

"Look at you!" the Elvenking said. "Here it is a beautiful day, don't you know, and you go and ruin it for everyone by demanding hard liquor at our beer-and-wine-only cookout! Is this true?"

Borin looked back at the king with equal sternness. "For that, you lock me up? It was just a misunderstanding! Do you have any idea how important I am? Did I mention that I'm starving?"

"And where" asked the king, "are your friends and so forth?"

"Probably in your forest, starving!"

"What were you doing in my beautiful Murkywood in the first place?"

"Starving, mostly."

"So you're a tough guy, eh?"

"I'm tough and starving."

"Well, okay then," said the king. "Guards, take Mr. Big Shot here and throw him in the pokey until he learns politeness. You'll have a nice visit with us yet!"

The elves locked him up and left him. They gave him plenty of beer and grilled meat. He had pork loin on that first night. It was a nice change of pace from eating strictly bread, or more recently, nothing. For a while, Borin considered telling them about the adventure, just out of gratitude.

Wood-elves are not cruel, even to their enemies, except for giant spiders, to whom they show no mercy. They are also merciless to goblins, rargs and trolls. But Borin, at least, was being treated mercifully.

Though the wood-elves treated him well, they thought they were being harsh. That's because of their essential wood-elf niceness. Compared to what Borin had been through for the last few weeks, he didn't feel harshly treated at all. He felt like he was being groomed to purchase a time-share.

There Borin lay, in a sparsely furnished suite with no mini-bar privileges. After the novelty of adequate food and drink wore off, Borin realized that his team might not be quite so fortunate. But he quickly said to himself "Oh well. What can you do?" It was not very long, though, before he was discovered by friends, but that's coming up in the next chapter. There, the wobbit will again show his usefulness, to Borin's great surprise.

Chapter 9

BEER BARREL BONDAGE

The day after the battle with the spiders, Bulbo and the dwarves put the last of their remaining strength into getting captured by the wood-elves. They were delighted to suddenly be surrounded by torches rather than bulbous glowing eyes. As the elves stepped forward, the dwarves weakly cried "Hooray!" They then put down their white flags and raised their hands above their heads. Since an elf is as skilled with a bow as a wobbit is with a cocktail shaker, the dwarves' only worry was that their surrender might not be obvious enough. Leaving nothing to chance, they all dropped to their knees.

Bulbo, on the other hand, decided at the last moment to pop on his ring and disappear. He ignored the otherworldly howling sound in his head and stepped out of the way. Instead of being forgotten by the dwarves, he was now being overlooked by the elves.

The elves must have had a busy day planned, because they marched the dwarves at a brisk pace. Bulbo could barely keep up as they approached the wood-elves' great, log-cabin-style lodge. There was a river that flowed in front of the place. The water flowed dark and strong, as espresso-like as the Magic River Of Sleepyness, but it was a different river entirely. This river wouldn't make you drowsy if you drank a flagon of it.

The dwarves were marched in at spear-point, and Bulbo scuttled in after them, in true wobbit fashion. The lodge was decorated in knotty pine paneling with furnishings that were made on the premises and sold in the gift shop. The elf-guards sang as they prodded the dwarves along. This didn't make being prodded along any less unpleasant.

In a great hall not too far from the lobby sat the Elvenking on an action recliner of carven wood and plaid upholstery. On his head was a bright orange hunting-crown, and in his hand was a tankard of lager, for autumn had come again. In the spring he would switch to a dopplebock.

The prisoners were brought before him, and he questioned them long and hard, but none of them yielded to his harsh probing. None of them were prepared to confess their real purpose of treasure-hunting, at least not while they were being questioned as a group. Given the opportunity, though, Loin and Groin were each secretly considering talking if an appropriate deal was offered. For now they all played dumb and refused to talk, remaining dopey and grumpy. Since they were now less likely to be shot by mistake, they were no longer acting grateful.

Fallin was the only one to speak, but he did so in true dwarf fashion. "How dare you question us like common criminals?" he said. "Do you have any idea who you're dealing with here? We're busy and important dwarves!"

"Sure, okay," said the Elvenking. "You dwarves are important and busy. Busy losing my savings in your so-called bank! And now, here you are in my vacationland, hunting my moose without a license. And did you think we'd like having you attack our barbecues, eh?

"Let me tell you, mister, here in Murkywood we try to get along with each other. None of that constant rushing around that you dwarves seem to enjoy. You come here with your massive, iron-bound wallets and your spoiled kids for one week a year and think you can tear the place apart. Well, we're still here when you leave, for Pete's sake!

"We wood-elves value your business as tourists, of course, but my guards tell me you're broke as well as rude. Did you think you could come here and take jobs away from my locals, eh? For crying out loud! You out-of-towners are too much! Well, we have some complimentary rooms for you folks where you can stay until you learn how to act politely and so forth."

111

He ordered that they each be put in a single room, sternly specifying that they receive no river view and no fruit basket. They were, however, each offered tennis lessons, a loaner racquet, and a spot in the autumn tournament. The Elvenking was a big believer in the rehabilitative power of exercise.

Room service brought them their first meal in days, a simple dinner of beer and sausage, with venison stew and a quail appetizer. Borin was having the same meal at the same moment, but the dwarves were not told that he had been captured too. It was Bulbo who found that out.

Poor Mr. Bunkins—never had he felt so weary and so alone, even when he was working for SmithiBank as a teller. Always wearing his ring, he hung around the lodge health club and the business center to kill time, but he was still miserable. There were hunting and fishing trips that he would invisibly join. Even though it was good to get out of the lodge, Bulbo always had a miserable time. Hunting and fishing were two things that Bulbo liked even less than riding on the back of an eagle. And he couldn't escape this way. Even though he could get out of the lodge, there was no escape from Murkywood.

There was plenty of food, since he had no qualms about stealing other people's room service. But there are only so many patty melts even a wobbit can eat, day after day. Bulbo was bored.

"I'm like an embezzler that's afraid to quit," he thought. He knew a teller a SmithiBank that had stolen a small fortune over the years, but had to keep working to keep hiding the evidence of his theft.

"I wish I was back in my studio apartment, away from all this plaid upholstery and knotty pine." He often wished, too, that Pantsoff were with them, if only to see the wizard get his comeuppance. Bulbo wanted to get home, but he knew Pantsoff would be of no use in making that happen. If there were to be any escape from the wood-elves, Bulbo would have to plan it, and lead the escape himself. He was, after all, a consultant.

Eventually, after a week or two of hanging around the lounge and eavesdropping on the bellboys, Bulbo found out where each dwarf was kept. He knew by including them in his escape plan they could create confusion that would improve his own odds of escaping, especially if the dwarves were caught. But still there was the problem of leaving Murkywood. He would never find his way out, with or without the dwarves.

Really, the only way to get home seemed to be by stealing at least some of the treasure away from the dragon, and then hiring a reliable guide and some bodyguards. Perhaps he could do it by sneaking into the service entrance, taking a few priceless odds and ends, and then getting away while the dragon was busy killing and eating the dwarves. Bulbo could then return to Wobbiton in style, hopefully before the dragon noticed that anything was missing. He needed the dwarves, so he steeled himself for another conversation with Borin.

Confinement was weakening Borin's resolve, so like Loin and Groin, he was close to telling the wood-elves everything. Then he heard Bulbo's cute little voice at the keyhole. Thus informed that he was not alone, he immediately became suspicious that one of the other dwarves might soon confess to the wood-elves. Bulbo was eventually able to get him to pay attention long enough to consider escape. Bulbo didn't have a plan yet, but since Borin never had any ideas of his own, he decided to await one from Bulbo. With Borin's authorization, Bulbo went to inform the other dwarves.

Bulbo brought encouragement to the rest of the company. He also brought Borin's angry instructions that everyone should keep silent about the treasure, complete with Borin's threats, accusations and insults. They were to await Bulbo's plan. Once Borin knew that Bulbo had evaded the elves in the woods, he became positive that Bulbo would be able to free them all, kill the dragon, and bring home the treasure. Borin would allow nothing to jeopardize this. Even if it meant that he would have to skip the Murkywood Lodge Autumn Tennis Tournament.

113

After years of Borin's abusive management style, the dwarves barely noticed the threats, accusations and insults. But they did each agree that the treasure was practically theirs already. They all stood by, awaiting the plan from Bulbo, quite happy to allow him to take care of everything. Incredibly, this was what Pantsoff had hired Bulbo for in the first place. So what was Bulbo's plan?

One day, while nosing about like a bored, invisible ferret, Bulbo discovered that the main lobby was not the only way out of the Murkywood Lodge. The Non-Drowsy Forest River that ran in front of the lodge had a tributary that wound around behind the lodge, a sort of riparian service drive. The rear of the lodge had a loading dock that allowed deliveries to be made by river raft. A portcullis secured the dock between deliveries. Just past the dock, inside, stood lots and lots of barrels: wood-elves, and especially their king, were very fond of beer. No hops or barleys grew in the area, so beer, and many other goods like pretzels, had to be brought in from far away.

As Bulbo crept about, secretly listening to the private conversations of others, he learned that many of the goods delivered to the lodge were from the Lengthy Lake, the original site of Lake City, near the Only Mountain and the corporate headquarters of SmithiBank. The new Lake City was a distribution center for beer and anything else the wood-elves wanted badly enough to pay for.

Barrels full of beer were tied together into great rafts and poled upstream to Murkywood. Afterwards, the empty barrels were generally tossed back into the river by the wood-elves, despite their reputation as environmentalists. The barrels would float downstream like huge pieces of litter until they returned to Lake City. There they would be refilled with beer, and sometimes washed out first.

For some time Bulbo thought about the portcullis. He took a long time to think, and he took a lot of breaks. Eventually, he decided that it was the only way the dwarves could escape, and soon he had the desperate beginnings of a plan. Desperate as it was, it was far better than any plan that Pantsoff had ever produced.

It came to Bulbo one evening as he was eavesdropping in the lounge. He was listening to an elf's monologue to a confidant about an embarrassing medical condition. Then he heard a bit of someone else's conversation about something less entertaining but more useful, so he gave it his full attention. It was the king's butler talking with the chief of the guards.

"Okay, so, come with me to the loading dock," he said. "We just got in a new shipment of beer for the party, don't you know. I'm working the third shift tonight, getting rid of some empty barrels, and I don't want to do it sober, eh? Let's you and me give that beer a taste."

"Some butler you are!" laughed the chief of the guards. "Doesn't the king usually have temps doing the grunt work?"

"It's the new cutbacks," said the butler. "The king told us we had to 'Do more with less. Work smarter, not harder.' We're still not sure what that heck he's talking about, eh?"

"Beats me," said the captain. "Let's go have a drink!"

When he heard this, Bulbo was all in a flutter, as Dorks often are, for it appeared that his legendary luck was still with him. He followed the two elves to the loading dock, where a barrel was immediately tapped and soon noticeably lighter. Luck of an unusual kind was with Bulbo then. The two elves quickly became stinking drunk. It normally takes a lot of beer to hammer a wood-elf, but this was special high-proof triple-bock sent all the way from the beer gardens of Far Anheuser to Murkywood for the king's own table.

The elves eventually passed out. In crept the wobbit, and soon he was scuttling away to the dwarves' rooms as fast as his stumpy legs could carry him. So it was some time before he arrived.

Bulbo didn't want to spend a lot of time explaining and defending his plan, so he avoided Borin's room and released Fallin first. Since wood-elf prisons are, like their lodges, run on the honor system, there were no guards. Fallin's dinner things had just been taken away by room service, and Bulbo knew that the elf with the book-cart

115

wasn't due to visit until tomorrow. He led the way to the next dwarf.

Soon there were twelve dwarves with Bulbo. It was a noisy procession, what with the dwarves constantly blowing their noses, adjusting their chainmail sweat socks, and dropping the tennis racquets that some of them insisted on bringing along. "Drat those dwarvish racquets!" Bulbo often said to himself. But they met no one as they walked, since most of the elves were off enjoying the annual Elf-Toberfest Beer And Sausage Bash in the forest clearing. They came to Borin's room last.

"Excellent work, Bunkins!" he said. "You may kill that dragon yet. Now then, tell us your plan!"

Bulbo told them the plan. The dwarves reacted as Bulbo had expected.

"Unacceptable!" said Borin. "Don't ever mention that plan again. Tell us your Plan B."

"Plan B?" said Bulbo. "You should be weeping with gratitude that I have a Plan A! Borin, you're the inventor of the adjustable rate mortgage, so maybe you have some ideas!"

"Um, well I, uh—" said Borin.

"I thought so," said Bulbo. "Unless you're prepared to apologize to the Elvenking, you'd better come with me."

Borin had never apologized to anyone, ever. He wasn't about to start now, even to win his release. Deeply irritated, he and the dwarves followed Bulbo to the loading dock.

The captain and the butler were still breathing, but out cold with no sign of reviving soon. At Bulbo's direction, the dwarves found thirteen empty beer barrels that they awkwardly climbed into, and Bulbo prepared to hammer a lid onto each one.

"Wait! How will we breathe in these things?" Borin asked. "There won't be enough air! We'll suffocate!"

"There are more than enough cracks and loose seams in these barrels to allow air in," said Bulbo.

"Then what will keep water from leaking in and drowning us?" asked Fallin.

"I'm pretty sure these barrels are all water-tight," said Bulbo.

"But that makes no—" said Borin, when Groin interrupted. "We could be sealed up for days!" he said. "We'll die of thirst!"

"Just drink a lot of water before I hammer the lids on," said Bulbo.

"Are you crazy?" said Fallin. "I've got a hyperactive bladder! What am I supposed to do?"

"These are all excellent questions," said Bulbo. "I'm sure that if you all apply some common sense on a case-by-case basis, you'll—"

"And who will let us out of the barrels?" asked Loin.

"No time to talk!" Bulbo said as he hammered. "Let's try to use some positive mental imaging and remain hopeful. I'll see you all soon!" With that, he pounded the last lid into place. Then he put on his ring.

Not a moment too soon! A number of elves came to the loading dock. They had already been enjoying Elf-Toberfest, so they were drunk and, predictably, singing.

"Oh, so what else is new, eh?" they said. "We have to interrupt our drinking to get more beer, and here we find the butler, drunker than we are! What do we do now?"

Even drunk, they figured out that the barrels to be taken up to the barbecue were behind the "empty" barrels with the dwarves in them. The easiest thing to do was to push the empties out of the way and into the river.

"These empty barrels sure are heavy," one said. "Are they really empty? Should we be dumping them? What if the butler gets in trouble, eh?"

"Who cares!" said another. "Serves him right! If he doesn't want a bad performance review, he should cut back the amount of drinking he does while on duty, eh? Maybe some singing will wake him up, and the captain, too." So they sang:

> *Roll, roll, roll away*
> *Gently down the stream*
> *Merrily roll barrels off of the dock*
> *While the butler dreams*

The barrels went into the water, and from there they drifted to the portcullis. It was at this moment that Bulbo discovered yet another weak point in his plan. Most likely you saw it some time ago and have been laughing at him. Or at least smiling smugly to yourself.

The problem with Bulbo's plan was that he was not in a barrel. How would he stay with the dwarves as they floated downriver? Who would let them out of the barrels? The dwarves would be trapped for who knows how long, to die horrible deaths by suffocation, drowning, or dehydration, or perhaps all three at once.

"More importantly," thought Bulbo, "how will I escape this lodge? Without the dwarves, how will I get home?"

It doesn't take much to get a drunken elf to sing, and soon the elves on the dock started in on another, louder song. Bulbo could barely hear himself scheme as they raised the portcullis, singing:

> Roll out the barrels
> We'll have a barrel of fun
> Float to Lake City
> To be refilled one by one
> Past giant spiders
> And webs that fill us with fear
> Send back barrels filled with peanuts
> And a lot more beer!

Panicking now, Bulbo jumped into the river with the last barrel and managed, despite his poor swimming, to catch hold of it and float along.

Out the barrels went, under the branches of the trees on either bank. The water and the air were both quite cold, which made Bulbo's back hurt more than ever. He became jealous of the dwarves in their cozy, warm barrels, deathtraps though they were.

As the night wore on, the barrels ran aground on the north bank of the river. Bulbo realized that they were no longer in the forest, but near an elf-village on its outskirts.

The two principal industries of the village were renting paddleboats and forwarding barrels to Lake City.

Elves came forward and soon the empties were tied together, to float the rest of the way to Lake City the next day. Wood-elves would accompany them to keep them from getting stuck along the riverbank. When they arrived in Lake City, they would collect a small cash deposit for each barrel. It wasn't much, but it was a living.

Bulbo knew none of this, but he took a chance and left the rafts to steal some dinner. He wondered briefly about the well-being of the dwarves, and then decided that they were still too close to Murkywood to reveal themselves and risk recapture. Not knowing when his next opportunity to release the dwarves might be, he decided he would have to wait and see. He quickly went back to eating his stolen tater tots and cocktail franks. A burgled bottle of peppermint schnapps made the night seem less cold. Soon he was asleep.

When Bulbo awoke, he did so with an especially loud sneeze. He stole an omelet, some coffee, a book to help kill time, and a hot water bottle, and then climbed aboard the dwarf-and-barrel raft. He ate for a minute, and then two elves climbed on and pushed the raft away from the bank with poles. They were underway.

Bulbo noticed that since he was wearing the ring when he stole the hot water bottle, it had become invisible too. Most things he held became invisible. But why didn't the barrel he was clinging to become invisible? Or if he had held hands with the dwarves during the escape, would they have become invisible? Then he wondered once more about weapons. The shovel he used to hit Gol-Gol had remained visible. He considered hitting one of the elves with the hot water bottle to see if it would become visible when used as a weapon, but decided that his experiment would have to wait.

Bulbo finished his invisible breakfast, which was difficult, like eating with your eyes closed. The barrel raft was headed towards the Lake, where Bulbo hoped to find locals that were either friendly, gullible or careless.

The dwarves had escaped the lodge of the Elvenking and were through Murkywood, but whether alive or dead remained to be seen. Bulbo was hoping they were alive, but he wasn't going to beat himself up if they weren't.

Chapter 10

HAPPINESS IS A WARM WELCOME

The day grew lighter and warmer as they floated along. Bulbo's mood, on the other hand, grew darker and colder. This was especially true whenever he looked up from his invisible breakfast on the dwarf-and-barrel raft, and saw in the distance The Only Mountain. Even after all the songs, stories, and haikus the dwarves had shared about it, he was not happy to see it. It looked tall and creepy, reminding him fleetingly of Pantsoff. Really, though, it could have been covered with butterflies and pizza, and Bulbo still would have felt uneasy. The prospect of having to break into a dragon's lair and kill him was not an encouraging one.

As the raft and the day crawled by, Bulbo amused himself by listening to the raft-elves talk, making sarcastic comments in his head. He never realized how much conversation there could be on the subjects of beer, hunting & fishing, and the pushing of barrel-rafts. The elves also spent a lot of time saying "gesundheit" to each other, whenever Bulbo sneezed. By the end of the day they still hadn't realized that neither of them were sneezing and that it was the Invisible Mr. Bunkins after all.

The elves talked endlessly about barrel-rafts, and the good old days of barrel-rafting back when SmithiBank was still based in the Only Mountain. Back then, the river was choked with barrel-rafts. Everyone had a job, everyone could get overtime whenever they wanted. As much as everyone disliked the dwarves and SmithiBank, they liked reminiscing about how great the economy was when they were still around. When Bulbo looked back on his time as a

SmithiBank employee, he rarely missed working there. Of course, it was better than being cold, wet, bored and uncomfortable, while facing an impossible task and certain death. On the other hand, he hadn't been trapped in a barrel for more than twenty-four hours. Thinking about the dwarves thus cheered Bulbo as the raft made its way.

The sun had set by the time they had arrived at Lengthy Lake. It was the largest lake Bulbo had ever seen, which was pretty much what he expected from its name. The dwarves had once purchased the naming rights and briefly renamed it SmithiBank Lake, but the name never stuck with the locals. They were happy to take the dwarves' money and put up a few signs, but they preferred simple, obvious names like Lengthy Lake and Lake City.

The locals were a practical-minded people, and by "people" I do not mean elves, dwarves, wobbits, or goblins, but Men, half of whom were Women. The failure of SmithiBank had been hard on them. They liked the dragon even less than they liked the dwarves. When a dragon burns down one's home and eats one's neighbors, one usually tries to learn from the experience. But the people of Lake City didn't learn the obvious lesson, which is to relocate as far away from any dragon as possible. But they did learn to make it harder for their new town to be burned, which they did by building it in the middle of the lake, accessible only by rope bridges and boats. They felt that building in the lake protected the town from dragon attack. This would have been true if the local dragon was of the non-flying variety, like a firedrake or a tyrannosaurus. Unfortunately, the dragon that destroyed their first town had wings and, unlike a chicken, it could fly. Perhaps they were hoping for the best, or perhaps they didn't remember the facts. Like the raft-elves, they too remembered the days of SmithiBank as prosperous, happy times. Memory can be very unreliable.

As soon as the barrel raft came within sight of Lake City, boats rowed out to retrieve it. Most of them would be refilled with Lake City Lager and then rowed back to Murkywood. The Lake people didn't actually brew all the beer. Some of it was made for them under license in the South and brought to Long Lake. The Southrons liked the larger market, the Lake Citiziens (as the citizens of Lake City called themselves) liked the huge mark-up, and the Wood-elves always liked more beer. The two elves that accompanied the raft quickly tied it off at the dock and went to town to enjoy some beer.

With the elves gone, Bulbo decided he could now safely open a barrel. He took off his ring and braced himself, expecting the worst as he looked in.

There was Borin, who was alive, mostly, but utterly miserable. If Bulbo had stuffed a dead Borin into that barrel and then opened it the next day, the smell couldn't have been any worse. Then Bulbo remembered that the dwarves had been on a diet of beer and grilled meat while imprisoned by the elves.

"Thank goodness your barrel was right-side up!" said Bulbo.

"If the dragon swallows you whole," said Borin, "and you come out the other end alive, you and I will be even." Bulbo saw no point in arguing. He helped Borin out of the barrel. Borin attempted to freshen up a little in the lake, while Bulbo opened the other barrels.

Fallin and Crawlin were the most unhappy, because unlike Borin, their barrels were upside down when the raft was assembled. Fortunately, neither of them had the strength to kill Bulbo then and there, despite their great desire to do so. Beefi and Bufu had somehow remained dry, but they were no more willing to help than Fallin and Crawlin. Wheeli and Deali came out healthy, but were also useless. Many of them had caught colds. They were sneezing, and clearing their throats more than usual.

"I hope I never smell weissbier again!" said Wheeli. "My barrel was full of the smell of it. What a horrible time! It was like trying to sleep on a frat house carpet. I'm gonna find a drink, any drink—but not a weissbier!"

Without any help and perhaps out of feelings of guilt, Bulbo opened the remaining barrels. Poor Fatso had to be spilled out rather than lifted, since he had put on a lot of weight while imprisoned. Tori, Rori, Gori, Loin and Groin were in barrels that had shipped a lot of water, so they smelled a little better, but were still wretched and vengeful.

They had avoided hypothermia despite the cold water, but were sneezing like the others.

"Well! Here we are!" said Borin, who was most confident when stating the obvious. He sniffed, cleared his throat, and then continued.

"Time for a meeting." Nobody spoke, or even sneezed, so Borin went on. "First, I'd like to request that all blood-oaths and promises of revenge against Mr. Bunkins be deferred for the time being. We all want to kill him, of course, but we still need him to break into our corporate headquarters and kill the dragon. And, more to the point, we need him to tell us what to do now."

"After everything you've been through," said Bulbo, "you still come to me for ideas?"

"Oh yes," said Wheeli as he coughed. "It's much easier to endure your bad ideas and complain about them than it is to come up with better ideas on our own." All the other dwarves heartily mumbled their agreement.

"And your ideas have all been better than Pantsoff's!" Deeli added. As miserable and near death as they were, they all had a good laugh about the poor job Pantsoff had done.

"Yeah, he's an idiot," said Bulbo as he sighed and wiped his eyes.

"So, now what do we do?" he said, rhetorically, but the dwarves leaned in with expectation.

"Well, we should head into town and tell them that you've arrived to establish the headquarters and first branch of the New Improved SmithiBank. They'll think the recession is over and the good old days are back again."

"Don't be ridiculous!" said Borin. "We're not ready to reestablish ourselves yet. All we want to do right now is get the treasure someplace safe. After that we can plan the formation of Smithi Financial Solutions. And when we do, we're certainly not going to establish it here in the boondocks. Besides, the Only Mountain has become a tomb for most of my friends and family. It'll cost a fortune to have all those bodies removed."

"Who's being ridiculous now, Borin?" said Deali. "You know as well as I that the dragon ate everyone. There'll be no bodies at all!" A long pointless argument was soon underway, to be broken up by Bulbo.

"Hey!" he yelled. "It doesn't matter when or where you rebuild. Just be sure to tell everyone in town that you'll be hiring and handing out contracts soon. They'll give us the celebrity treatment at no cost as we re-supply and get our strength back."

"Ohhh!" said the dwarves, as they gradually understood. True to their word, none of them had an idea that was better than Bulbo's. Borin, Wheeli and Deali got up and went with Bulbo into the drab town. It was entirely made up of small, fire-resistant buildings, docks, and bridges. They soon were stopped by some guards, who were astonished at the dwarves' filthy condition.

"Who are you and what do you want?" they shouted.

"I am Borin Oakmanfield, CEO of the New Improved SmithiBank to be known as Smithi Financial Solutions. I have returned!"

"Oh please!" said one of the watchmen. "You're not Borin. You look like you've been cleaning out the stables with your beard. Smell like it, too."

"How dare you!" said Borin. "Here, you fools. Take my card!" As they looked at the damp card, Bulbo interrupted.

"I am Bulbo Bunkins, a consultant for Mr. Oakmanfield," he said. "What my employer is trying to say is how happy he is to be back on the shores of Lengthy Lake. More importantly, he's looking for enthusiastic professionals to help him get his new bank going.

"You two look pretty sharp," he continued. He was ignoring the fact that each of them had more tattoos than teeth. "Would you be interested in becoming Branch Managers?"

A crowd was starting to gather, since there wasn't much entertainment in Lake City. A large, red-faced watchman came forward. There was a Deputy's badge on his chest.

"Good evening, gentlemen," he said to Borin and Bulbo. "We know who you two are, so who are your filthy friends?"

"They are Wheeli and Deali," said Borin, as all three of them sneezed. "Sons of my father's daughter."

"They're who, now?"

"He means they're his nephews," said Bulbo.

"You must be very proud," said the Deputy. "Let's get the lot of you off the street before there's complaints. We'll see about cleaning you up, getting a hot meal into you, and then hurrying you out of town."

"No, No, No!" said Borin. "We are busy and important dwarves! Well, except for the little one, of course. He's a wobbit. Now take us to the Mayor immediately!"

"Help yourself," said the Deputy. "You four bums go have your big meeting with the Mayor. He'll have you thrown out of town without a cleanup or a meal. Just don't mention that you talked to me first." He led the way to a restaurant nearby. Diners and waiters looked up and wrinkled their noses as the dwarves walked through, headed towards a banquet room in the back. They entered the room, and were suddenly standing among the Mayor and some relatively prosperous-looking Lake Citiziens.

Borin sniffled, and then cleared his throat pretentiously. "I am Borin Oakmanfield, CEO of the New Improved SmithiBank, to be known as Smithi Financial Solutions. I have returned!"

Everyone looked at Bulbo and the three filthy dwarves for a moment, and then burst out laughing.

"No, really, I am!" Borin said. He was fuming. He started to get out his business cards.

"Oh criminy" someone said in the back. It was one of the two raft-elves. "You're supposed to be back in the hoosegow at our lodge! The king is gonna have a conniption fit"

"Does anyone here speak wood-elf?" said the Mayor loudly. "I can't understand a word this yokel's saying!"

"The head dwarf is Borin Oakmanfield," said the other elf. "He's escaped from the Murkywood Lodge, where he was being held for moose hunting without a license, disturbing the peace, inciting giant spiders to violence, and conspiracy. The same goes for the other two. I'm not sure about the little one. How did you folks escape then, eh?"

126

"Is this true?" said the Mayor. His eyes lit up at the chance, however unlikely, that Borin was telling the truth. "Has SmithiBank returned? Are you hiring? Are you taking bids from your suppliers? Will you be relocating here? We have some excellent commercial real estate available, and a lot of quality workers, too!"

The mayor was very excited with the prospect of reducing unemployment, stimulating the downtown business area and rebuilding his tax base. He didn't wait for Borin's response. He was already imagining the New Lake City. They could use beautiful, flammable building materials, and put it all on dry land, too. Anything was possible now! Borin's return was the best thing to happen since the Mayor took office. He would leave a legacy of Rebuilding And Prosperity.

The wood-elves would have to be handled, of course. It was unfortunate that Borin had become drunk and disorderly, or whatever, in their kingdom, but the elves would get over it. They always did in the past. And when the good old prosperous days were here again, there'd be plenty of money to go around. The elves would benefit just like everyone else. His wonderful reverie was interrupted as singing broke out in the banquet room.

> *The dwarves went back to their mountain*
> *The dwarves went back to their mountain*
> *The dwarves went back to their mountain*
> *To see what they could see*
>
> *To see what they could see*
> *To see what they could see*
> *The dwarves went back to their mountain*
> *To see what they could see*

So they sang, or very like that, for the rest of the night. The lyrics were typical of the Lake City people and their literal-minded lack of creativity. But everyone had a good time, even the elves. The dwarves were treated as guests of honor, and Bulbo was treated like a strange friend that had been brought along, uninvited, to the party.

127

The other dwarves were eventually rounded up at the dock, bathed, and brought to the banquet. That night they were comped at a nearby inn, and the next day a modest villa was made available to them.

Whenever a dwarf came to the gate for a delivery of pizza or Southron Fried Chicken, the gawkers and autograph-seekers would start singing. They would sing if they heard a dwarf sneeze. The songs usually featured two lines or less, repeated endlessly, always referring to the return of prosperity for all, thanks to the dwarves.

The dwarves had their old clothes destroyed and new ones were provided by a local shop that specialized in clothes for husky boys. Their beards were trimmed and highlighted. No dwarf had ever been this popular, certainly not in the days of the old SmithiBank. Despite their colds, they took to smiling and laughing, sometimes even in public. They came to be regarded by the locals as happy and sneezy.

Life was so pleasant for the dwarves that their discussion of revenge against Bulbo eventually stopped. They even took to drinking his health. Bulbo had never been this popular, either.

The raft-elves soon were ready to return to the Murkywood Lodge. Their barrels were thoroughly sanitized, de-dwarfed, and refilled with beer. Even though the wood-elves are very casual, the guards at the lodge had, by this time, discovered the escape of the thirteen dwarves. I have never heard what happened to the chief of the guards, but the butler went into a rehab program and eventually got his job back.

The Elvenking had been so furious at the escape that he forgot to say "thankyou" to one of the guests at checkout. He calmed down later, when his raft-elves returned and gave him their news.

"Well okay then!" he said. "That's why you were so quiet about your business! We'll see what happens, Mr. Big Shot Oakmanfield, when you settle into Lake City again. How are you going to do business west of town without going through Murkywood, eh? Where will you conduct your annual meetings without my lodge? We'll get an apology out of you yet, and a polite one, too!"

At the end of a fortnight, which is what they call two weeks in Lake City, Borin realized he should strike while the iron was hot. So he spoke with the mayor and his aldermen, and said that soon he and his company must go on to the Only Mountain.

Then for the first time the Mayor realized that before the prosperity of the old days could return with the New SmithiBank, Smog the Dragon would have to be dealt with. He had been swept up in dreams of wealth and commerce, but he hadn't given any thought to Smog. He assumed that a dwarf as big and important as Borin would have a foolproof plan.

"Of course we'll be happy to outfit your expeditions, Mr. Oakmanfield. If you have an army coming, we can make arrangements for their lodging and provisions. Or perhaps you've hired a celebrity warrior-hero? We'll do everything necessary to indulge his various heroic appetites, while preserving his privacy at the same time. What'll it be?"

"No, no we won't need anything like that," said Borin, sniffling, "just provisions and supplies for the fourteen of us."

"Ah!" said the Mayor. "The wobbit is some sort of secret weapon! I suppose wobbits kill dragons the way mongooses kill snakes. Brilliant!"

"No that's not it at all!" said Borin. "The wobbit, Mr. Bunkins, is a burglar. He'll be entering our offices by stealth."

"Very good," said the Mayor, "and then what?"

"I'm not sure. We suspect it will involve burglary."

"Burglary? You're going to have one wobbit steal the treasure, and bring it to you, piece by piece? An army of wobbits might do it over a few decades, but eventually Smog would notice that his treasure was being carried away! He'd kill all of you. That's your plan?"

"No. Mr. Bunkins is our consultant and he's creating a plan, even as we speak."

"Really? Whenever I see him, he's either drinking or staring at the Mountain with a desperate look in his eyes."

"Yes. That's his style," said Borin as he sneezed. "He ponders for quite a while, and then he becomes a blur of activity. That's how he planned our escape in the barrels!"

"Mr. Bunkins came up with the barrel plan?" said the Mayor. At that moment, he gave up all hope in Borin's adventure, the return of SmithiBank, and any chance at the wealth he had been imagining. He realized that the money spent entertaining Borin & Company was gone forever, but there was no sense in dampening the excitement that had swept through the city. People were hopeful, and spending money again. He didn't want to end the boom prematurely. And there was a chance that Smog had died on his own, or had flown away long ago. Anything was possible, after all. The Mayor tried to remain encouraging.

"In Mr. Bunkins' capable, well-marbled hands, I'm sure your adventure will succeed. Just let us know what you need, and Lake City will provide it. We have always valued our relationship with SmithiBank and its board members. I'm sure you will look to us as you prepare for the launch of Smithi Financial Solutions."

So one day, although autumn was now getting on, three large boats left Lake City, loaded with rowers, dwarves, Mr. Bunkins, and many provisions. Ponies, not quite as small as the last two sets of ponies, were sent ahead to the landing place. The Mayor, his aldermen, and many Lake Citiziens bade them farewell, singing repetitive, obvious songs. Bulbo still had not come up with a plan.

"Did anyone remember to bring swords?" asked Fallin.

Chapter 11

ON THE DOORSTEP, UNDER THE MAT

They spent three unhappy days traveling by boat up the Lengthy Lake. It was cold, unpleasant and boring, much like the dwarves themselves. The only thing to look at as they rowed was the Mountain, which looked taller and creepier the closer they got. When they disembarked, they saw some new fairly small ponies, complete with provisions and necessaries, but no new paraphernalia.

They spent a cold and lonely night camped at the landing, and their spirits fell even lower. That morning they set out northwest, slanting away from the River Runny and drawing ever nearer to the creepy Mountain.

The next day was colder and lonelier and their spirits fell again, like a wobbit on skates. They knew they were drawing near to the end of their journey, and they could no longer ignore the fact that they still had no plan. Even more depressing was the scenery. All around then, the grass was scorched black. The trees looked like they had been bitten off at waist-height, as if their foliage had been dipped in cheese sauce and eaten like gigantic broccoli.

They reached the Mountain all the same, without any sign of the dragon other than the compulsively thorough destruction that surrounded his lair. They made camp, and the next morning Borin sent Bulbo to scout SmithiBank's entrance, especially the area to the south where the reception desk once stood. He was to look for signs of the dragon. With him went Fallin, who had sharp eyes, and Wheeli and Deali who had even sharper eyes and were far younger. Their youth and lack of seniority was important. If necessary, Smog could be tricked into eating them while Fallin and Bulbo escaped.

At a place called Parrot Hill, very near the Mountain, they hid behind a blackened rock and peeked nervously at the Mountain's dark opening. There the River Runny splashed ominously past the reception desk. A massive, iron-bound sign hung above: "SmithiBank, Little Earth's Premier Mortgage Lender." An old promotional banner hung alongside. At the top it said "CD Rates of 5.00% - The Best In Town!" The number was crossed out and underneath was successively written and crossed out "3.00%," "1.00%," "0.25%," and finally "Free Gift - Inquire Within!" The iron-bound sign bore the smashed imprint of a huge tail. The banner was torn in several spots, as if by gigantic claws.

Out of the opening came a dark smoke. Nothing moved, except the water, the smoke, Bulbo, and the dwarves. There was no sound, except the water and the nervous chatter of Wheeli.

"No signs of the dragon that I can see! Nope, there's no dragon here!" he said. "Let's head back to the camp. This must be the wrong mountain."

"If there's no dragon, what's causing the smoke?" said Bulbo.

"Maybe it's from a hobo's campfire," said Fallin.

"What's that smell?" asked Deali. "It smells like the Reptile House at the Iron City Zoo."

"Come on, guys," said Bulbo. "The smell and the smoke are from the dragon. He's in there, so we can head back. I've seen enough."

"You're the consultant," said Fallin. "You must know what you're talking about. Let's get out of here."

*   *   *

With thoughts of zoo-smells and despair, they made their way back to the camp. Borin had the other dwarves trapped in a dinner meeting. They were passing his map back and forth, brainstorming ideas on where the service entrance might be hidden. Groin was looking at it.

132

"It looks like it might be right near the top of the mountain," he said.

"Of course not!" said Borin. "Stop being an idiot! Loin, it's your turn!"

"It must be at the bottom, on the other side, to the north," Loin said, trying to sound confident.

"Horrible idea!" said Borin. "Stop wasting our time! Fatso, take a look!"

"Um, maybe it's halfway up?" he said, wincing.

"You're wrong, all of you!" said Borin. "These are the worst ideas I've ever heard!" Borin wasn't very good at brainstorming. He stopped when he saw Bulbo's group come back from their scouting mission.

"Ah, our consultant has returned. Mr. Bunkins, you have all the answers. Where do you think the service entrance might be?"

"Don't you want our report on the dragon?" said Bulbo.

"Please, Mr. Bunkins, let's stick to the agenda," said Borin. "We'll review your findings at our breakfast meeting tomorrow as planned. Until then, just do as you're told. We're busy and important dwarves."

"Fine," said Bulbo. "I'm going to bed. Tomorrow I'm going back to the mountain to find the service entrance. Having just been there, I can tell you it's no picnic. It was as cold, tiring and difficult as a last-minute Derwin's Day shopping trip. It looks like Smog the dragon is still there, so tomorrow's trip to the Mountain will be dangerous, too. I'll need some volunteers to come along, just in case I get eaten, to bring the news back to Borin."

No one volunteered.

"Of course, we will be leaving at first light, and returning after last light, or perhaps at first dark. If you're on my team, you will be unable to participate in any of Borin's meetings tomorrow."

Everyone volunteered.

"Not so fast!" said Borin. "We can't all be running off with our merry consultant on his nature hike. There's work to be done here, real work: thinking, talking, looking at maps. Wheeli and Deali, neither of you are of any use to me here, so go with Mr. Bunkins and good riddance. It'll serve you right if the dragon eats all three of you."

"What about me!" said Fallin. "Bunkins needs my sharp eyes."

"Oh, will you stop with the 'sharp eyes' already!" said Borin. "I need your sharp eyes right here, to review today's minutes for misspellings."

"Great elephants!" muttered Fallin. This was odd, because he usually avoided swearing.

"You've all become quite worthless," Borin said. "I move that we adjourn this meeting for the night and reconvene tomorrow morning at breakfast. Who will second the—"

Everybody loudly seconded Borin's motion.

"Motion seconded," said Borin. "All in favor say—"

Everybody said "Aye!" loudly, in their most impatient and bored voices.

"It's unanimous," said Borin. He then added as he always did, "All opposed?"

This was Borin's way of monopolizing a last few, precious moments of his employees' time. There being no votes against, he grudgingly hammered his massive, iron-bound gavel on a makeshift podium of piled rocks.

"Meeting adjourned,' he said, as the group dispersed. They quickly found their tents and immediately pretended to be asleep, to discourage any further "offline meetings" that Borin sometimes attempted.

Bulbo and his team woke early the next morning to make absolutely sure they wouldn't be called into another of Borin's dreadful meetings. The dwarves tiptoed barefoot, waiting to put on their palladium-toed boots until they had crept quietly out of camp.

Walking near the Mountain was like marching in a gigantic ashtray. Everything on or near the mountain had been burned, and many of the larger boulders had been clawed. Smog appeared to have eaten all the trees, which he preferred well-done, or perhaps *en flambé*. Ash got into the dwarves' boots, and soot got all over everything. Still, they

134

all were delighted that they were avoiding Borin's meetings for the day.

Bulbo decided to start exploring, once again, at the front door. From a distance, all they could see was the smoke, the sign, the promotional banner and the river that ran in front of it all. Wheeli and Deali insisted on having a tick-tack-toe contest to see who would go in for a closer look. After a half-hour of stalemates, Bulbo gave up and walked toward the gate himself. At that point, he would have walked straight into Smog's mouth.

Soon he was close enough to look into what once was the main entrance of SmithiBank. He saw the reception desk on one side, and the velvet ropes leading to the teller windows on the other. He also saw a sign that directed "All deliveries in rear" with an arrow pointing to the other side of the mountain.

Bulbo took his team in the direction of the arrow until they were on the other side of the mountain. There they spent the rest of the day searching for a door. While Wheeli and Deali looked under small rocks, Bulbo discovered a singular area of vertical mountain wall. Deciding that he had found the only possible spot for the service door, Bulbo brought the dwarves back to the camp, where the dinner meeting was just beginning.

"Great news, Borin!" he said. "I've discovered where we'll find our door!"

"Do you mind?" said Borin. "We're trying to have a meeting!"

"I yield the floor to Mr. Bunkins," said Beefi, who was just getting started. "In fact, he can take my spot on the agenda. I've got no progress to report anyway."

"No progress!" said Borin. "How will we ever find the door with that kind of attitude? Am I the only one here who cares about getting into the Mountain?"

"Would you like my report?" asked Bulbo patiently.

"Yes, yes, go ahead," said Borin.

"Well, as I said, I've found the spot where the door must be located. It's at the back of the mountain."

"I knew it!" said Borin.

"Hey!" said Groin. "That's where I said it would be, in our meeting yesterday!"

"Oh, stop it," said Borin. "It's clear that the wobbit and I deserve all the credit. Please continue with your report, Mr. Bunkins."

"Again, the door's in back, so we need to move our camp there and await Derwin's Day."

"Relocate our camp? Why?" said Borin. "What are you talking about? And what does Derwin's Day have to do with anything?"

"We all have to camp near the door," said Bulbo, "so that on Derwin's day we're all available to help open it, if necessary."

"I'm still not following you," said Borin.

"Oh, come on!" said Bulbo. "Don't you remember our talk with Enron?"

"Who?"

"Enron! The guy at the Hidden Valley Ranch! He showed us the moon-jumble on your grandfather's map!"

"Oh, the half-elf," said Borin. He had the unfortunate habit of pointing out the race of any non-dwarves. "We had a meeting with him. What of it?"

"Enron told us the map says that we have to 'Stand by the service entrance when the parrot knocks, and the setting sun with the last light of Derwin's Day will shine on the key-hole.' We have to be waiting there, ready. Derwin's Day is sometime next month, right?"

"Wrong again, wobbit!" said Fallin. "Derwin's Day is tomorrow."

"Tomorrow?" said Bulbo. "We almost missed it! Wasn't anyone keeping track?"

"Mr. Bunkins," said Borin, "we can't remember every detail of this project for you. As our consultant, you have to take the initiative once in a while."

"Even though I'm the only guy here who doesn't celebrate the stupid holiday?" said Bulbo. "This adventure depends on our entering the Mountain, which can only be done at one spot, and only on Derwin's Day. But I have to force you to be at the right place at the right time? Don't you care?"

"Of course I care," said Borin. "It's just that we all figured you'd probably end up using the main entrance instead."

"Oh, so that's what you figured?" said Bulbo. "I hate to disappoint, but there's no way I'm going in through the front door! That's probably where the dragon's waiting. So if you want to get into the mountain any time before Derwin's Day next year, you'll pack up your fairly small ponies with your provisions and necessaries, and we'll head over there immediately!" Bulbo turned and stomped away.

"We haven't adjourned yet!" said Borin.

The camp was broken down, packed and moved that night. It turned out that all the dwarves were keenly aware that the next day was in fact Derwin's Day, but they had long forgotten its significance to their adventure. All they could think of regarding the special day was the most venerated dwarf tradition of all: the Derwin's Day White Elephant Gift Exchange.

The Gift Exchange traditionally involved dwarves getting together at work to fight over near-worthless "gifts." Each dwarf would provide the cheapest or least-desirable gift they could find. They then took turns either opening a wrapped gift, or stealing a gift that someone else had already unwrapped. The idea was to get the "best" gift out of all the wretched refuse available.

This event was an intense combination of all the things that dwarves treasure most: inflexible rules, the abuse of authority, getting a good deal, intimidation, bearing grudges, defeating your enemies, cheating your friends, acquiring objects, and randomly assigning value.

To Bulbo it was all quite ridiculous. But the morning of Derwin's Day, the dwarves lost all interest in avenging the deaths of their families. There was no thought about regaining the unimaginable wealth the dragon had stolen. Instead, all they could talk or think about was the Gift Exchange.

When Bulbo saw the gifts themselves, it made all the excitement seem even more ridiculous. Wobbits will hoard almost anything, but the gifts presented there, in the shadow of the Only Mountain, were rubbish even to Bulbo. Being exchanged were: 1) a cloth with the old SmithiBank logo on it, used for polishing massive, iron-bound wingtips, 2) a little pad of stolen return address labels that read "Bulbo Bunkins, Bug End, Wobbiton, 3) a wallet card tip-calculating table, with the tips figured at either two or three percent, 4) a washcloth from the Hidden Valley Ranch, 5) a goblin-made brass pinky ring with the stone missing, 6) a small bag of used golf tees, 7) a pair of pine cones from the Rargs' meeting place, 8) a stale loaf of Bjork's honey-wheat bread, 9) a broken beard trimmer, 10) a wood-elf moist towelette picnic pack, 11) a Lake City Chamber Of Commerce map of their downtown shopping area, 12) a seasonal necktie with a pattern of little Derwin portraits, and 13) a scorched rock that had obviously been picked up and wrapped just before the Exchange.

The gifts were crap, although not literally, as is often the case among rural dwarves. The Exchange eventually ground to a halt and the dwarves spent the rest of the morning either boasting of their success or planning their revenge at next year's Gift Exchange. After lunch, Bulbo took Borin to the sheer rock at the Mountain's base where he knew the service door must be. The two of them stood there for a moment.

"Now what?" said Borin. "Do you expect me to just stand here and wait?"

"Actually, yes," said Bulbo. "This is where you have to be to open the door. The setting sun will shine on the keyhole."

"Nonsense! I've got meetings to lead and reports to review! I can't just wait here!" said Borin. And then for emphasis he added "With you!"

"No problem," said Bulbo. "Leave the key with me and I'll open the door."

"Not a chance!" said Borin. "This key is mine, and I'm staying right here." He sat on the ground with his arms folded. So did Bulbo. They looked at each other silently.

Then Bulbo spoke up. "If only Pantsoff were here," he said.

Borin responded "Yeah. He'd know what to do." They both laughed uproariously, united in their feelings about the wizard.

"Do you really think a parrot will show up and knock at the moment the keyhole appears?" asked Bulbo.

"If you can believe the half-elf's translation of my grandfather's map," said Borin, "then yes, I guess so."

"But a parrot?" said Bulbo. "Around here?"

"Oh sure!" said Borin. "There used to be lots of parrots. Lake City was once home to a booming exotic pet industry. It was the wonder of Little Earth. Derwin himself was said to own a massive, steely-eyed macaw."

"That's amazing," said Bulbo. They made small talk until they both fell asleep. Bulbo napped well into the afternoon. He woke in a panic, sure that he had missed the parrot and the keyhole. Then he realized that the sun hadn't set yet.

He heard a strange noise behind him. He turned and saw that it came from a brightly colored parrot, looking out of place in the cold, ashen waste. The parrot spoke.

"Knock knock!" it said. "Knock knock! Knock knock!" over and over again. It woke up Borin.

Suddenly Bulbo understood. "Who's there?" he replied.

"Panther," said the parrot.

"Panther who?"

"Panther no panth, I'm going thwimming!" said the parrot. "Awk! Thwimming!"

Bulbo didn't normally like talking birds, but he was impressed that this one could tell a joke, use the correct timing, and perform the fake lisp that the joke required. It was a joke that was insensitive to anyone with a lisp, and as a Dork, Bulbo had many lisping relatives. He tried to not be offended.

"The bird must have picked up that joke from the insensitive dwarves of old," Bulbo thought, until another sound interrupted him. This one was an otherworldly "Zap!" that came from low in the cloudy skies. A single ray of light from the setting sun shone through the clouds and fell on the rock wall.

"Look at that beam of light," said Borin. "How odd that it should make a 'Zap' sound. Or any sound at all."

"Never mind that!" said Bulbo. "The key! The key! Get it now, while there is still time!"

Borin got up unsteadily and patted himself down like he was trying to find a pack of cigarettes. He dug deep into his pockets and found the key.

The spot where the light fell slowly started to glow. A keyhole appeared. By the time Borin got out his key, the keyhole was glowing like a Jimi Hendrix poster under a dorm-room black light.

Borin tried the key, but couldn't turn it. He removed it, turned it over, and tried it again, and it turned. The outline of a doorway appeared, as short and wide as the dwarves that made it. Borin pushed madly at the door, but it wouldn't open.

"Let me try," said Bulbo. He turned the key, held it in the keyhole and pulled. The door slowly pulled open.

The other dwarves came up from the camp to see what was happening. Everyone gathered at the open door and looked in. The darkness inside was so dark it made the night sky look bright by comparison.

"That's dark!" said Fallin.

"Why is everyone looking at me?" Bulbo said.

Chapter 12

INSIDER TRADING

For a long time the dwarves stood motionless in the dark before the door. They assumed that if they waited in silence long enough, Bulbo would do something, like come up with a great idea or risk his life on their behalf. Bulbo wasn't doing anything or saying anything either. Of course, it was Borin that spoke first.

"Quiet, please. Take a seat everyone. Now is the time for our esteemed Mr. Bunkins, who has long enjoyed our protection, our discounted meal program and the free use of our gear—now is the time for him to perform the service for which he was engaged as an independent contractor and consultant. Now is the time for him to become a Burglar."

Bulbo interrupted, to keep Borin from going on like this for the rest of the night.

"You're saying that you expect me to go into this extra-dark passageway first?" he said.

"Oh no, not at all," said Borin. "We expect you to go alone!"

Bulbo was not surprised by Borin's attitude, nor would be anyone who knows dwarves. The most that can be said of dwarves is this: they are cheap, pompous, boring, and they have repulsive personal habits. But at least they weren't trying to mislead Bulbo, and he knew it. It's true that dwarves are dishonorable and indecent, but they are never disappointing if you don't expect too much.

Not wishing for any additional ceremony, Bulbo stepped into the service entrance and began his descent. "Let's get this over with," he said.

He put on his ring and took out his Elf Army Knife as he walked. He opened what he hoped was a truly deadly blade, but ended up with the leather-punch. "This will be handy if I'm attacked by a horde of were-wallets," he thought. "Which one of these gadgets is for killing dragons? Maybe the metal file?"

He decided on the large blade, which had served him so well in his fight with the spiders. It was glowing, anticipating the fight with Smog.

"Oh, great. I'm invisible, but carrying a completely visible, glowing weapon. Well, whatever. I'd never survive a fight with a dragon anyway." He folded the blade away.

"Best to just stay invisible and be as quiet as possible. Smog won't even know I'm here." Then he went to put his knife in his pocket, but missed. He dropped the knife, kicked it by mistake, picked it up, dropped it again, swore loudly, picked it up again, and went on.

"If only I could wake up in my recliner with a cocktail by my side," he said. But he did not wake up. Although his reality was nightmarish, it was unfortunately not actually a nightmare. This discouraged him, but he kept walking.

The cool pitch-darkness started to become warmer and less dark as Bulbo descended. The darkness was giving way to an unnatural greenish glow. The silence was giving way, too. Bulbo noticed a sound other than his internal dialogue. It was a gasping, gargling, strangling sound. Then it stopped. Bulbo stood still and held his breath. After a few moments, it started again. "That's the worst sleep apnea I've ever heard," he thought.

As he kept walking further forward and downward, the green glow became more distinct, the snoring became quite loud, and the warmth became uncomfortably hot.

"I wish I'd dressed in layers," he thought as he unbuttoned his waistcoat. He was getting a little sweaty as he walked. He saw a doorway at the end of the passage. The heat, glow and snoring were all coming from the room ahead.

It was at this point that Bulbo stopped. Going on from there was the bravest thing he ever did. Bulbo hadn't done many brave things, it's true, but going forward in this situation would have been brave for anyone. Except for

142

Pantsoff. In his case, going forward would have been considered an act of foolishness or self-delusion. Pantsoff might easily miss the obvious signs that the dragon lay ahead. But in Bulbo's case, though, it was truly bravery. He had not missed the signs: the heat, the glow, and the snoring of Smog!

There he lay, a vast green-gray dragon, fast asleep. Wisps of smoke came out of his flared nostrils and from under his huge pointy overbite. Beneath him, his arms and great front claws were folded as if he were an immeasurable praying mantis. All about him were piles of precious things, sets of commemorative coins, checkbooks, mint condition action figures, and bearer bonds, all green in the nauseous light.

Smog lay partly on one side, so Bulbo could see all of the office supplies and furnishings that had fused to his burning underbelly during his long rampage through the SmithiBank headquarters. Adjustable ergonomic desk chairs, gold pen sets, jeweled ashtrays, and massive, iron-bound paperweights all were crusted over his long, pale belly.

Bulbo gazed at Smog and the treasure. It was like reading tabloid headlines while in a checkout line. He wanted to look away, but couldn't. For what seemed like an age, but for what may have only been half an age, he kept gazing. Finally, he remembered why he had come to Smog's lair in the first place. He scuttled invisibly across the floor among the treasure-mounds and heaps of office furnishings. He saw a jeweled battle-axe, a common item in any dwarf office. He grabbed it off the pile, but when he saw the ax was floating in front of him, he was reminded once again that weapons don't become invisible. He quickly set it down and grabbed a great, two-handed coffee cup instead. As he picked it up, it vanished. He was relieved until he noticed Smog. The dragon stirred a wing and his snoring changed its note, from G to A-flat.

Bulbo ran furiously but went nowhere for a moment, until his large, bare feet finally got traction on the carpet and he fled. The next thing he knew, he was approaching the top of the tunnel, the service entrance, and the dwarves. He still had the cup. He removed his ring.

"You're alive!" the dwarves all shouted. Fatso was delighted, but the others sounded more surprised than pleased. Borin doubted that Bulbo actually got to the treasure-room until he saw the cup and claimed it for his own. As he directed Bulbo to start recovering the rest of the treasure, a vast rumbling woke in the Mountain underneath.

Borin's greed quickly gave way to cowardice. He and the other dwarves began to look back and forth at each other and Bulbo, waiting for someone else to come up with a good idea that would save them. They knew the rumbling must be the dragon. Pantsoff's failure to include the possibility of a live dragon in his project plan was no longer a hypothetical error, but a real-life disaster. Removing a vast treasure from a dead dragon's lair was challenging enough, but stealing it from a live dragon was something else entirely.

Earlier, Smog had heard someone telling a distant knock-knock joke, and then felt a draft, and then heard a clumsy clattering, and then a furtive scuttling. He soon was fully awake, and felt like having a nice snack. He was about to get himself some villagers and milk when he realized something was missing. The cup!

Unfathomable! How dare anyone steal the treasure that he had rightfully stolen from SmithiBank, who had themselves stolen it from their customers? Who would do such a thing? He thought he had eaten all of SmithiBank: its employees, officers, and managers. Was it the people of Lake City? But why? What had he ever done to them, other than burn down their homes and businesses? Everyone always blames the dragon!

That was when Smog rushed out the main entrance and flew blazing into the air. He circled the mountain and settled at the top in a terrifying yet dramatic spout of green and red flame. The dwarves peeked up from the boulders where they were cowering, and saw the whole thing. As they futilely attempted to burrow to safety with their bare hands, Bulbo dashed back into the service entrance, something the dwarves were still afraid to do.

Bulbo realized the only thing worse than facing Smog with the dwarves would be to face him all alone. And either of those things would be worse than the other things Bulbo discovered he disliked, such as flying, or hunting and fishing. Bulbo stopped reviewing his many dislikes and called to the dwarves.

"You idiots! Into the service entrance! The dragon's lair is, ironically, the only place where we're safe from the dragon!"

"Fatso!" cried Borin. "Bring the ponies!" Since Bulbo had proven that he was no longer expendable, Borin had identified a new patsy. He figured that Fatso might keep the dragon busy for a few moments while more important members of the company ensured the continuity of the project through the current disaster. But Fatso ignored Borin and rushed slowly to the service entrance, wheezing and clutching his chest. The ponies remained at the campsite, facing a sad but certain future. Smog looked down upon them as you or I might look at a tray of appetizers.

"We're way over budget for ponies on this project," said Borin, to no one in particular. Fortunately, most of the provisions and necessaries had been saved.

Smog circled the Mountain a few more times. He went with his hunch that someone from Lake City had stolen his cup. He would eat the thieves and burn them and smash them, and then eat them some more. Revenge! But first, back to bed to sleep off the ponies he'd eaten. And then, tomorrow night, Revenge!

Smog slept and morning came. The dwarves felt their terror grow less, but their despair grew more. They had no idea what to do next. All night they had argued plans back and forth, but each plan included a task titled "Kill The Dragon" for which they had no ideas at all, much less any actionable steps.

"This is all my fault, really," Bulbo said. "I should have known that warning you about this weak point in your plan months ago would not be enough. It was foolish for me to expect that one of you might come up with a way of solving this problem."

"You finally understand us, then," said Borin. Dwarves don't always "get" sarcasm. "You're the consultant. Let's hear your recommendations."

"Yes, recommendations," said Bulbo. "Why don't I go see if Smog is sleeping again. If he is, I'll try to find a weak point in his armor." He waited for someone to talk him out of this suicidal plan, but no one did.

"I suppose I'd better get started soon. 'The early wobbit catches the wyrm,' as the Old Dork used to say whenever he got up before 10:00."

"Sounds good, Bunkins," said Borin. "Now get going. We'll be waiting back at camp. I have to prepare for a meeting."

"You're going outside? That makes no sense!"

"Oh, please!" said Borin. "If we hear the dragon killing you, we'll have plenty of time to come back in. Don't worry about us."

"No, I won't," said Bulbo. He turned, and soon he was scuttling down the tunnel, invisible and trying very hard to not drop anything or sneeze.

When he found himself outside Smog's chamber, he saw that the dragon lay motionless. The snoring sounded different than before. There was no sleep apnea. Instead it sounded deliberate, almost cartoon-like. There was a rattly in-breath, followed by a clearly whistled exhalation.

"Could he be pretending to be asleep?" Bulbo asked himself. "Who would do something like that?" Then Smog spoke.

"Well, well! If it isn't the Prince Of Thieves! I can smell exactly where you are. Your breath is horrible, and I'm an expert on horrible breath. What did you have for breakfast? A raw onion?"

"Um, an omelet, actually. The onions were supposed to be caramelized, but they were little undercooked. There may have been some garlic in it too. It's actually a funny story, you see—"

"Silence! You bore me! Now then, who are you and what do you want? If you'd like to give me some hints, I'll be happy to try to guess your name. I'm quite good at it."

"No, thanks," said Bulbo. "I'm in a bit of a rush."

"Fine, have it your way!"

"My name is Bulbo Bunkins of Wobbiton, and all I want is a look at you, O Chairman Of The Board."

146

"Yes, well, I am magnificent, it's true. Was it worth the long, lonely trip from Wobbiton to see me, Bingo?"

"My name's Bulbo, and yes, seeing your magnificence was definitely worth the trip. It wasn't a lonely one, though. I traveled by pony with thirteen dwarves. Borin & Company, of SmithiBank." Bulbo wondered if he was perhaps telling the dragon too much.

"Dwarves!" said Smog. "Lake City ponies ridden by dwarves. That would explain the ponies' aftertaste. I thought perhaps they had the mange. Tell me, Mr. Funkins, how do you like working for Borin? Has he given you a performance review yet?"

"The name's Bunkins, and no. I was supposed to meet with Borin last week. He had to cancel at the last moment, and hasn't rescheduled yet."

"Of course! Not to worry, Mr. Bunkhouse, whether the dwarves discuss your performance with you or not, they'll find a way of cheating you out of your bonus."

"Bonus? No one mentioned a bonus—"

"Excellent! I couldn't have done a better job myself! No bonus for you, Mr. Bumbershoot, but plenty for them, I assure you. It's business as usual for the dwarves. They've stuck with the same key principles since the first dwarf crawled out from under the first rock. In fact, I used to correspond with the first dwarf. His name was Derwin, although I never had a chance to eat him. By the way, if you came from Wobbiton, tell me, however did you get through Murkywood? The Elvenking isn't exactly a big fan of dwarves."

Bulbo laughed. "Oh Smog, you should have been there! The Elvenking captured and imprisoned the dwarves. I was never caught so I came to the rescue, hiding all thirteen dwarves in barrels. They spent two nights floating down the River Runny!"

"Hilarious! Sorry I missed that! The revenge of the Barrel-Hider! You know, Borin's gang sounds like another gaggle of dwarves I ate once upon a time, but I can't remember the name of their bank."

"It was SmithiBank, O Great And Powerful Smog. Borin and his dwarves are the current SmithiBank board of directors. You ate all the other officers and employees when you burned the old Lake City and moved in here."

"Yes, of course, SmithiBank. And they expect you to kill me and bring them back their treasure, I suppose? Is that it? Speak up, you assassin!"

"We're not sure of the plan's details, actually. Right now they're letting me take the initiative."

"Initiative?" said Smog. "You're taking all the risks, you mean. It's a perfect arrangement for Borin. He can blame you for the poor planning when his charade finally fails altogether."

"Yeah," said Bulbo. "That's how it looks."

"And you're just going to take their abuse? Poppycock! Show some self-respect, Bumpo! Tell me where they are, I'll eat them, and I'll hire you. You can polish my silver or something. You'll be alive, and working for an employer that appreciates you. Give it some thought!"

Bulbo considered Smog's offer carefully as he pretended to listen. But he couldn't bring himself to betray Borin & Company, not like all the other times. He knew he couldn't trust them, but he was fairly certain they wouldn't eat him. On the other hand, he was positive that if he accepted Smog's offer, the dragon would end up eating him sooner or later.

As he daydreamed through Smog's rant about the dwarves, he recalled that he was supposed to look at Smog's underbelly for a weak spot. As Smog gestured grandly Bulbo could plainly see a spot near his left armpit that was completely bare. A flipchart easel that once stuck there had long since fallen off!

Bulbo now had the exact information that he came for. Time to go! He didn't want to interrupt Smog's monologue, and he was still invisible, so he snuck away without saying anything. In mid-sneak, he knocked over a set of collectible decorative plates. They commemorated the annual dwarf Commercial Lenders Of The Year for the last two hundred years. Bulbo wasn't able to enjoy their fine workmanship, though, because the great shattering crash they made startled him and alerted Smog of his escape attempt. Bulbo ran for it.

148

"Come back here Barrel-Hider! You wretched homunculus! You're missing the offer of a lifetime! No one walks away from a deal with Smog! I will not be insulted! You're ruined! I'll kill you! I'll eat your dwarves and burn Lake City again! Come back here! Come back!" He blew great gusts of green flames after Bulbo. It was a poor way to convince him to come back.

As Bulbo ran for his life, he thought, "Never knock down a dragon's knick-knacks!" and it became a favorite saying of his later, although now it is remembered as "Never pay for a service agreement on a major appliance."

As soon as the wobbit returned to camp that afternoon, Borin demanded a full report. Bulbo took a minute to decide which details to leave out and which weak points to improve. Then he presented his edited account. The old parrot that told the knock-knock joke fluttered over and started staring at him.

"That bird might be smarter than the dwarves, and he's certainly listening more closely," thought Bulbo. "I can't have him calling me a liar."

"Beat it, Polly!" he said quietly. "Stop staring into my soul and revealing my innermost secrets!" He threw a rock at it. Unlike countless giant spiders, the parrot dodged the rock easily. It perched again and continued to listen. Bulbo picked up another stone to try his throw again.

"Stop it, you moron!" said Borin. "The Parrots Of Lake City are good and friendly. This is a very old bird. He could be the last descendant of Derwin's famous parrot. They were a long-lived and magical race, and this might be one of those that can remember SmithiBank as it was before Smog. Perhaps he was witness to the dragon's terrible attack."

"That's all very interesting, Borin," said Bulbo. "Did you still want my report?"

"Yes, yes. But quit throwing stuff at the bird!"

So Bulbo told them about his conversation with Smog, or at least the parts that wouldn't get him into trouble. "I feel that he may have somehow guessed that I was accompanied by all of you. And he seemed to suspect Lake

149

City of helping us, too. We have to warn them that he may be heading their way looking for revenge."

"That's out of the question," said Borin. "The people of Lake City know the risks of living near a dragon. But they refuse to run away, unlike the prudent SmithiBank survivors." All the dwarves took a moment to be proud of their running away years ago.

"If he attacks them," said Borin, "that's the way it goes. They can take care of themselves. It's too bad they don't know about the bare spot on his office-supply-encrusted armpit. If they did, at least they would have a fighting chance."

"What's for dinner?" he said, to no one in particular. The parrot spread its old but colorful wings and flew away.

As they dined on granola bars, Bulbo gradually realized the danger of sitting in the open at the foot of a mountain that had an insulted and angry dragon inside. He voiced his concern, but Fallin boasted that he would see Smog long before the dragon could see them.

"Besides," he said. "What are the chances that he'll come back to attack us at the same spot? It's like lightning striking twice!"

Bulbo forgot about the dragon, confused by Fallin's poor analogy. The dwarves were discussing how they would spend their shares of the treasure. When Bulbo asked how he was to get his share home to Wobbiton, he was met with angry stares. Shipping the treasure would be a complicated, expensive undertaking. It was another part of the project that remained unplanned by Pantsoff. The dwarves obviously didn't want to talk about it.

The talk turned instead to the great horde itself. Legend had it there was still an armory of dwarf-made super-premium spears, commissioned by the Mad King Blagohair, but never paid for. By the time it was ready for delivery, King Blagohair was imprisoned for demanding kickbacks on earlier government contracts for scimitars, bucklers, and gauntlets.

They discussed other treasures crafted by the dwarves of old. There seemed to be a great many items that had never been shipped to the purchasers. Most of the treasure, though, was deposited by SmithiBank customers to be kept safe and to earn the famous Compound Interest Of The Dwarves. There were magnificent, mint-condition bow and arrow sets, shields that were double-forged and fully krausened, and suits of armor with the price tags still on them. There were many sport coats of armor, and khaki pants of armor, too. But fairest of all was the great white gem, so huge and pale and fabulous that it drove dwarves mad with desire: The Delta Burkenstone!

"The Burkenstone! The Burkenstone! Do you hear an echo?" said Borin. "I'd give the lives of all of you just to gaze on its thousand facets!"

"That reminds me," said Bulbo, "we've really got to get below before we're all killed. I'm not kidding."

Ever since Bulbo rescued the dwarves from the giant spiders, then led their escape from the wood-elves, found the entrance to their treasure hall, and discovered the one weak spot on Smog, the dwarves were starting to take him more seriously than they did back in Wobbiton. They still treated him like a sneaky outsider, but they did listen to his advice. Bulbo was no longer just a former teller. He was truly a consultant. After some argument from Borin, which was just to keep up appearances, they all headed into the service entrance.

Bulbo left nothing to chance. He pulled the stone door, and it closed with a snap and a clang. "Those stone doors! I would have expected a clunk and a kaboom."

"Yes, Mr. Bunkins," said Borin. "Thanks to you, we are now trapped in the Mountain with Smog!" The door had no knob or even a keyhole on the inside.

As Bulbo mentally prepared his rebuttal, a terrific kaboom shook the Mountain. Everyone knew it wasn't the belated sound of the stone door closing. It was Smog attacking the Mountain itself!

Smog smashed the mountain with his tail a few more times and then breathed fire on it to keep in practice. He had just missed Bulbo and the dwarves, and he was furious. Smashing and burning made him feel a little better.

"You've escaped my wrath for the moment, Mr. Brighto Buckskin. So until I catch up with you and your

151

dwarf accomplices, I'll destroy Lake City again. I'm sure they're mixed up in this as well. Ta-ta for now!"

With that, Smog belched into his palm. After extinguishing his burning hand, he politely said "Excuse me" and flew away south to Lake City.

Chapter 13

HOME ALONE

"You've doomed us all, you pin-head" Borin said. "Are you in league with Smog? Bunkins, I'll kill you!

Bulbo slipped on his ring and ran for his life down the long hall. He felt it very unfair that he was being accused of cooperating with Smog. He regretted disclosing as much information as he had, but now was not the time to argue such subtleties with Borin.

The dwarves were closely pursuing Bulbo, and there was only one place he could go: towards the treasure and, possibly, Smog.

Soon there was no hallway left and Bulbo had no choice but to run into the treasure hall.

The treasure room, like the hallway, was darker than any darkness Bulbo had ever seen. Smog and his ambient green glow were gone, which meant Bulbo wouldn't be eaten, but also meant that he couldn't see a thing. Not even the stack of gold pieces he tripped over. He fell, and decided to lie still. Maybe the dwarves would rush past him and Bulbo could avoid being killed.

The dwarves came in, and Borin started micro-managing right away.

"Loin and Groin, get some torches lighted! Fallin, Wheeli and Deali, keep a lookout for the Dragon. Everyone else, help me find that miserable wobbit. I want him captured alive, so don't—"

Borin stopped talking as soon as the torches provided some light. All he could think about was his sudden view of the treasure room, jam-packed with more valuables than he

153

had seen in years. The long-lost Assets Of SmithiBank! He sat down and started digging his hands into the treasure all around him, like a kid in a sandbox. The other dwarves forgot about Bulbo, the dragon, and everything else as they vacantly staggered about, scooping up jewels and coins with both hands.

Sensing a change in the dwarves' mood, Bulbo took off his ring, grabbed a torch from Groin, picked up a silver serving tray, and quickly scuttled to the top of a hill of treasure. It's not easy to sled with a burning torch in hand, but Bulbo did it. He wanted to try to keep the dwarves' mood light. It worked. Everyone laughed, so Bulbo climbed to the top and sledded again, this time down the other side of the hill.

At the bottom of the treasure hill, on a small heap of staple removers and binder rings, there it sat. Bulbo guessed it from Borin's description. He had found the Delta Burkenstone. It was indeed fabulous and gigantic. Bulbo was enchanted by its round, sassy, magnolia-white radiance. He dropped his torch and reached down with both hands to pick it up. He held it briefly, like a cold, flint-hard bosom.

Bulbo realized that he should hide this luxurious object away, and quickly. Borin might feel somehow entitled to the Burkenstone, and Bulbo didn't want there to be a misunderstanding between them. Nor did he want to be killed. He remembered how upset Lady Gol-Gol had become over the loss of a ring. Borin might be a poor sport, too. Whatever happened to "Finders keepers, losers weepers"? Besides, Borin had hired Bulbo as a burglar, so why shouldn't he burgle, just this once?

As Bulbo lusted after the Delta Burkenstone, the torch he dropped suddenly went out like an unattended cigar. Even though it wasn't quite as dark as before, it was still pretty dark on the far side of the treasure hill with no torch-bearing dwarves nearby. Unlike all his previous wanderings in the dark, this one left Bulbo disoriented. He tried to find his way back to the dwarves, but soon realized he was walking in circles. The delicious weight of the Burkenstone held him anchored on one side. Rather than releasing it from his sweaty grasp, he kept it hidden in his waistcoat and called out to the distant dwarves.

"Help! Help! Borin! Fatso! Somebody! Help!"

"Now what?" said Fallin to Borin. "What's bothering our consultant?"

"It can't be the dragon," said Borin. "Bunkins would be dead already. Unless Smog is torturing him, to trick us into coming forward. I'd better stay here. Take Crawlin and go see what's wrong."

They climbed the treasure hill and then ran down on Bulbo's side yelling "Whee!" Neither Crawlin nor Fallin believed the dragon was anywhere nearby, and they were still giddy with treasure-lust. Bulbo was delighted that someone had actually come to help when he called. He had to fight the urge to gush, "I found the Burkenstone! I found the Burkenstone!"

He could barely keep their attention anyway. Fallin was admiring some ivory backscratchers, and Crawlin was headed towards a display of bronzed baby shoes. Borin yelled from the top of the hill "I'm King Of The Dwarves!" and sledded down on an unobtainium shield into a pile of jade coffee stirrers. He walked up to Bulbo.

"Any sign of the Burkenstone?" he asked.

"What?" said Bulbo. "No! Of course not! Why are you accusing me?"

"Bunkins, I've got something for you.

Bulbo flinched, expecting the worst. When he opened his eyes, Borin was handing him something.

"An advance on your pay. It was part of an order of armor we got from the wood-elves years ago. They never paid the shipping and handling, so we never delivered it. It's a First Class Mailshirt. Try it on! I'd keep it myself, but it's a little tight across the chest."

Bulbo took off his waistcoat and tried on the armor. It fit pretty well.

"Is there a mirror here?" he asked. There were none. Somehow, that was one of the few treasures that neither SmithiBank nor the dragon had accumulated.

"Unbelievable! No mirrors! I would have expected a whole wall of silver mirrors in adamantium frames."

"You're not at a Potato Republic store, Mr. Bunkins. Trust me, though, you look great. And that's some excellent armor. First Class Mailshirts are made out of Invincibilium. It's completely arrow-proof, and it resists wrinkles."

"Dry clean only?"

"Oh no! It's machine washable and pre-shrunk. You look great in that color. Really, that shirt is you! And don't forget the matching helmet." He gave it to Bulbo, who put it on. "Very sharp! I've never seen you in a coordinated outfit. It makes you look very professional. Great for job interviews. Now, did you want me to wrap that up, or will you wear it home?"

"I must look like a Goblin Wars re-enactor," said Bulbo. "I think I'll just slip my waistcoat on over it."

"As you wish," said Borin, and he wandered off. He glanced around furtively, as if he were looking for porn or a deep-fried Twinkie. But he was looking for the Delta Burkenstone, and he would not find it.

The other dwarves were busy for hours, having the time of their lives. Beefi and Bufu were stuffing their pockets with sapphires. Tori and Rori were throwing bundles of strapped elf currency at each other, having a money-fight. Each time a bundle hit, the strap would break and paper money flew everywhere, as the dwarves hooted with glee.

Bulbo, on the other hand, was becoming bored with all the valuables. He had seen enough, he had shoplifted the Burkenstone, and now he was starting to think about food again. "I would give a good many of these solid-gold runcible spoons to try a sporkful of chili back at Bjork's compound."

"Borin!" he called out. "You've all armed yourselves with swords made entirely out of freshwater pearls, and your armor is so gaudy you look like the chorus from a disreputable operetta. But how will we get out of here? Not the front door?"

"Heavens no!" said Borin. "I'll lead the way out. I know the SmithiBank offices like the back of my hand! Thanks again for finding the service entrance that I knew nothing about."

"Don't mention it," said Bulbo. Borin looked around and then said, "Yes, this is the way! Just like I remember! Come on, everyone, follow me!"

After backing out of a few dead-end hallways, and opening a few closet doors by mistake, they headed down a long, broad corridor. Everywhere they went had been blasted and befouled by the dragon.

"What unsanitary habits!" Bufu said. "Without any treasure around, you really notice the smell."

The company all agreed to keep moving quickly to get away from the workplace-refrigerator stench. Borin took them through a door too small for Smog to squeeze through. They entered a vast low-ceilinged room filled with cramped cubicles.

"These are the Great Cubicles of Floor, my grandfather."

"They don't look that great," said Bulbo.

"Of course not," said Borin. "But they represent great savings for SmithiBank. My grandfather was a genius at reducing costs. He doubled the number of bookkeepers that were crammed into this space. Once upon a time, workers wasted countless hours stretching and turning around. But Floor's improvements made those things impossible!"

As they passed through, the company had to step gingerly over piles of skulls and bones.

"Hmm. Smog didn't burn or eat these employees," said Borin. "He probably had them trapped and they starved to death once the snack machines were empty. They must have suffered for weeks. I hope they remembered to punch out on the time clock."

They exited the office into another large hallway where Smog had passed. His filth was everywhere.

"And I thought pigeons were dirty," said Beefi. "How many more of these disgusting hallways do we have to walk down? When will I be able to clean my boots?"

"I've got a rock in my shoe!' said Gori.

"We've been walking forever!" said Tori.

"Yeah!" said Rori. "When are we gonna get there?"

"We're there!" said Borin, as he opened another door. The company stepped out into daylight again. They had spent all night frolicking in the treasure piles.

"This is a look-out post," said Borin, waving at the binoculars and sandbags.

"In the old days we had guards at posts like this all over the Mountain. They were crewed by our most trusted and reliable family members."

"Really!" said Bulbo. "Why didn't they warn you that Smog was approaching?"

"This may have been the problem," said Borin, as he opened another door leading back into the mountain. Inside was an opulent barracks, with a fully equipped kitchen, a bumper pool table and game area, and several couches facing a wall of windows.

"Here, our high-performing relatives could keep watch from inside, warm and relaxed under richly-deserved quilts. Our old theory was that being comfortable would help us to stay alert. In retrospect, that may not have been a good idea. Let's camp here.

"Hey, Borin," said Bulbo. "There are lookout posts like this all over the mountain, right?"

"Yes, dozens."

"And they all have doors that lead into the mountain, right?"

"Of course! How else would the lookouts communicate with upper management in the event of a hostile takeover or attack?"

"So there were dozens of doors into the mountain other than the service entrance that I risked my life to find?"

"Well, yes, I suppose so," said Borin.

They all settled in. Bulbo looked for food in the kitchen, but there was only *crap* and water. (If you want to know what *crap* is, I can only say that it's like a cross between Rye Krisp and cocktail pumpernickel. It's made by the people of Lake City, and they put so many preservatives in it that it lasts forever. They sell it, but never eat it themselves.)

The company snacked and rested and napped as the dwarf guards of old. Bulbo looked up from his couch, his mouth filled with *crap*, and wondered aloud "Where is Smog?"

"Maybe he's gone forever," replied Borin. "He's not here, and that's all that matters."

Chapter 14

BOURBON AND WATER

Where was Smog? How hard is it to keep track of a gigantic, flying monster that roars, breathes fire and glows in the dark? The dwarves, as you would expect, didn't know and couldn't be bothered to find out. In Lake City, however, everyone knew exactly where Smog was. He flew there right after smashing the hidden service door to the Only Mountain.

As a rule, the Lake Citizens spend as little time as possible looking at the Only Mountain. In the heyday of SmithiBank, it was always festooned with huge banners and billboards insisting that the reader refinance their mortgage, or at least open a home equity loan. Even without the ugly advertising, the Mountain was dreary and at the same time, uncomfortably pointy-looking. Once SmithiBank was gone, looking at the Mountain made the Lake Citizens think about its new resident, Smog. which they preferred not to do. Finally, any mountain on a totally dark night is not much to look at anyway.

This one particular night, however, two people were looking at it. The Mayor happened to glance up at the Mountain as he stepped out of a quiet cocktail lounge for a smoke.

"Hey!" he said. "There's a light on the Mountain! Borin and his dwarves have begun work on re-opening SmithiBank! They must have killed the dragon! Quick, call my press agent! Lake City is coming back! Hey Bart! Isn't it unbelievable?"

"Yup," said Bart, the town's sheriff. He was looking at the Mountain, too, while out doing his rounds. He had been squinting at the lights for some time, with eyes as clear and cold as a pair of high-quality ice cubes.

"Yup," he repeated. "Unbelievable. I don't believe it at all. That light's not from Borin. That's from the dragon."

"What?" said the Mayor. "The dragon? Come on, Bart. Stop kidding around. You've got to be more positive! Your bad attitude is going to hold back our Lake City redevelopment!

"The dwarves must have had some sort of actionable plan after all! With SmithiBank in business again, I can lead Lake City to a brighter tomorrow! I can be Mayoral! I'll be Mayor for the rest of my long life, and I'll leave an unparalleled legacy. SmithiBank is back!"

"Nope," said Bart. "That's the dragon." His mouth barely moved when he talked, which he did infrequently and quietly. A lifetime of lonely toughness had left his face so chiseled and his features so hardened that you could have cracked walnuts on his cheeks. But nobody ever did. He called over his Deputy, and then spoke to the Mayor again.

"If that press agent of yours owns a bow," Bart said, "you'd best tell him to bring it. You might want to fetch yours as well, Mr. Mayor, while I cut the bridges. Deputy, sound the alarm."

"No, no, no!" said the Mayor. "Don't sound the alarm! You'll create a panic! And don't cut the bridges, either. That defense is only for attacks by werewolves or bogeymen. Get a grip on yourself, Bart. You're paranoid! You're hysterical!"

Bart looked back with no emotion in his eyes. "Do I look hysterical?" Bart wasn't used to polite conversation. His longbow, which he always carried, did most of his talking for him, except when ordering at restaurants. It talked for him, and sometimes with him when he was especially lonely. From time to time, the arrows would join in the talk, too. He didn't talk to people much, but they talked about him constantly. They called him Bart The Bowman, with typical Lake City practicality.

Bart looked at his Deputy, who said, "Sounding the alarm, Bart!" as he ran over to a huge gong and started whanging away at it.

The Mayor glanced around nervously at his constituency as they came out of their homes, taverns and all-night diners. They gathered around the gong, awaiting an explanation.

"And now, a few words from our sheriff," said the Deputy.

"To arms!" said Bart. "Smog!"

Nobody moved. Like the Mayor, the people of Lake City had been thinking only of a prosperous future since the dwarves' earlier arrival by barrel. Once they figured out what Bart was talking about, they couldn't believe it.

"You heard the Sheriff!" said the Deputy. "Run home and fetch your longbows. We'll make our stand here, with Bart The Bowman."

The people still didn't move.

"Look!" said the Deputy. "Here comes the dragon!"

The light that had occasionally flashed in the distance now was much closer. It was no longer flashing, and it had become distinctly dragon-shaped. As one, the people wailed in terror and ran for the nearest boat or bridge, abandoning Lake City.

"Do you think they'll be back with their weapons?" said the Deputy to Bart.

"Nope," said Bart. Bart was still squinting towards the dragon. "It's just you and me." He turned to his Deputy and saw him running for the docks, trying to catch one of the last boats. Bart didn't normally spend much time on regret, but he wished that he had cut all the rope bridges before sounding the alarm. Instead, he was left to fight Smog alone. On the other hand, he wasn't especially comfortable around people. He was at his best when it was just him and his bow. And his arrows.

The dragon approached Lake City and began to circle in preparation for his attack. He looked down and smiled.

"Excellent!" said Smog to himself. "One worthless little man! They call this a defense? Balderdash!"

Bart watched as the dragon circled. Keeping his eyes on Smog, he drew his ivory-handled longbow. Without looking, he fitted it with an arrow. It looked like the dragon would soon appear at the far end of Main Street to line up on Bart and make his deadly power-dive.

Suddenly, something colorful fluttered to Bart's shoulder—an old parrot. Irritated that a bird got the drop on him, Bart tried to scare it off but it stayed, and spoke to him.

"Knock knock!" said the parrot in its old, creaking voice.

"I'm a little busy," said Bart.

"Knock knock!"

Bart decided to play along, if only to get rid of the bird. "Who's there?"

"Ivanna."

"Ivanna who?"

"Ivanna tell you how to kill Smog!"

Bart ignored the sheer stupidity of the joke and tried to make the most of things. "Well? Go ahead and tell me. The dragon will be here in a moment."

"Shoot your arrow at the bare spot in the armor on his left armpit! Awk!"

"His left, or my left?"

"His left, like I said! The right side, as you look at it! Here he comes! Awk! Can you see the bare spot?"

"Yup."

"Good luck, Sheriff!"

"Luck? Being as this is a six and a half foot yew bow with a ninety-eight pound draw, the most powerful longbow in the world, and can put an arrow clean through any armor, it's Smog that's got to ask himself one question: 'Do I feel lucky?'" Bart really liked talking about his bow.

The bird flew to safety as Bart selected a different arrow. Now that he knew of a critical target on the dragon, he decided to use a special arrow, an arrow that would really make an impression. The arrow had a brilliant silver head.

"Arrow!" said Bart. "Lucky Silver Arrow! I have saved you for this moment. Years ago my grandfather, Burt The Bowman, shot you at a dragon but missed, and was torn by its mighty claws. My father, Brett The Bowman, retrieved you and shot you at the dragon but it bit his head clean off. And now I, Bart The Bowman, have my chance with you, my ancestors' Lucky Arrow."

163

Smog reared back in the air and hovered for a moment, to taunt Bart before eating him. "Talking to your weapon? You're certifiable, you pathetic hominid! Say goodbye to your bow!"

Encouraged by the clear view of Smog's left armpit, Bart shared a few last words with his best friend. "Speed well, Lucky Silver Arrow. Make my day."

Bart's bow twanged like a mighty country-western singer. The arrow sped straight to its target. No roll-on deodorant ever found an armpit with greater accuracy. It buried itself in Smog's massive underarm, found his heart, and the dragon knew he was done for.

"Egad! I'm done for!" the dragon said. As he died, he shot back and forth across the sky, sputtering, like an over-inflated balloon suddenly released. He gained altitude briefly, and then collapsed onto the town. He thrashed back and forth until every last building was flattened. A loud groaning of overburdened wood was followed by a long, splintering crash. Lake City and Smog sank to the bottom of Lengthy Lake.

The Lake Citiziens turned back from their rout at the sound. They saw their city vanish into the lake with the dragon. The danger was over, so they started complaining. They caught up with the Mayor, who was leading the retreat.

"Some legacy you've left us! When we elected you, we had a drab city in the middle of a lake. Thanks to this administration, we now have a drab city at the bottom of a lake!"

"Come on, good people, please!" said the Mayor as he was being surrounded. "This is great news! We've killed the dragon!" Then he smiled to himself, suddenly realizing that "Smog is dead, and his treasure unguarded!"

His constituency quickly brought him back to reality.

"It was Sheriff Bart that killed the dragon. If only he had not been smashed and drowned in the wreck, we would impeach you and legitimately elect him our new Mayor! All mourn Bart The Bowman, lying dead at the bottom of Lengthy Lake."

"Nope," said a quiet, confident voice from the edge of the crowd. A soaking wet Bart stepped forward. There was

164

lake-weed in his hair and a fish-tail flapping from his pants, but he somehow looked imposing as always.

"I'm alive, and Smog is dead," he said. The townspeople cheered. Bart took off his boots and poured the water out of each.

"Bart for Mayor! Bart for Mayor!" cried the townspeople. The Mayor knew he had to act fast, so he stepped forward to shake Bart's hand.

"Bart, on behalf of a grateful town, let me extend our thanks. Your enthusiasm will be very valuable as we build our new Lake City. It will be the regional center of industry and commerce, and a destination resort. But before we begin building, and before any talk about recall elections, let's figure out who's really responsible for the destruction of our homes and businesses. Certainly not me, your humble public servant. So who's to blame?"

After a quiet moment, someone hesitantly said "The dragon?"

"Well, yes," said the Mayor, "the dragon is responsible, in a way, but why? Who roused him from his peaceful slumber? Who goaded him into attacking us? Who took advantage of our good-natured generosity? Who never once paid a bill or picked up a lunch tab or left a decent tip? Who's short, bearded and smells of beer?"

"The dwarves!" said the townspeople. "Kill the dwarves!"

"Hold on, folks," said Bart. "Before we talk about who's going to kill who, let's look at the facts. There's no way the dwarves are still alive. Smog ate them first, as soon as they stumbled into him.

"It's time for two things. First, we need to care for the women and children. Start by building some shelter and looking for food. Second, we'll need help from our neighbors, so I'll contact the wood elves as our ancestors did, by messenger parrot. Let's get to work."

And so it was that word of Smog's death reached the wood-elves. Of course, the parrot told the news to everyone he met on the way there and back. Everyone he told went on to tell someone else. He somehow let the news slip out to some Murkywood spiders. He also mentioned it in confidence to the Viscount Of The Eagles while catching up on old times in his eyrie. Bjork got the news from two of his talking dogs as they were setting his place at the dinner table. They probably heard from their disreputable cousins, the rargs, who heard from the spiders and in turn told Blog, son of Agog, late Gobfather of the Moisty Mountains. Enron picked up the rumor, which was soon all over the Last Waffle House. Bulbo's landlady, Virginia, was there for a spa treatment, and she took the news all the way back to Wobbiton, but told no one. Through all of Little Earth, only Lady Gol-Gol remained completely in the dark about Smog's death.

As they got the news, everyone immediately had the same realization that "Smog is dead, and his treasure unguarded!" At that, each of them made a plan of their own, however unlikely, to get a piece of that treasure.

In the meantime, the Elvenking of Murkywood sent to the people of Lake City such relief as he could: government cheese, second-hand mobile homes, and plenty of beer, all by river-raft. He also sent a host or two of wood-elf warriors, each armed with a traditional razor-sharp hockey stick and wearing a terrifying goalie mask. It wasn't quite cold enough for them to ice-skate up the river, so they swiftly made their way on foot.

The Elvenking and his host were welcomed as liberators. He met with the Mayor, and they soon negotiated a two-way split of Smog's treasure that made everyone happy.

The elves accompanied Bart and the Lake City militia as they began their march to the Only Mountain. Once there, all they had to do was stuff some sacks with treasure, bring home as much as they could carry, and repeat steps One and Two until the treasure was gone. At least, that was the idea.

Chapter 15

CLOUDY WITH A CHANCE OF BATTLE

Now we will return to Bulbo and the dwarves. They were trapped. Not in the Only Mountain, but in another of Borin's interminable meetings.

"Next on our agenda," said Borin, "is the matter of transport." As always, Borin alone had a copy of the agenda, which allowed him to do anything he wanted in his meetings for as long as he wanted. Fallin rolled his sharp eyes at yet another agenda item.

"How are we to get all this treasure to our home in the Ironing Board Hills?" Borin said. "Bulbo, what did Pantsoff have planned?"

At the mention of Pantsoff's now-legendary "plan" for the adventure, everybody had a good laugh. Borin didn't normally incorporate humor into his meetings, but just this once he was in an especially good mood. He was surrounded by treasure. In fact, he was sitting on a pile of white gold lip rings and ear cuffs. They were destined for the gift shops of the Hidden Valley but were never shipped, due to some problems with the paperwork.

"But seriously, Bulbo," said Borin, "what's your plan for moving all this treasure out of here?"

"Back in Wobbiton," said Bulbo, "I'd usually rent a big wagon, buy a lot of beer and invite some buddies over without telling them why." He was stalling. Bulbo had been asking himself the same question, but had received no answer. He was now rich, but only in a theoretical sense. How would he ever be able to enjoy his wealth? He didn't want to resettle in Lake City. Being the only wobbit for miles made him lonely. He was tired of always being the shortest guy in the room.

Before a realistic plan could occur to him, an old parrot fluttered into the treasure chamber, the same bird that disclosed Smog's weak spot to Bart The Bowman. He landed on Fallin's shoulder and began pecking at his long Van Dyke.

"Hey!" Fallin cried. "Stop that!" The parrot stopped pecking and looked him in the eye.

"Knock knock!" croaked the bird.

"He's trying to tell us something!" said Borin. Everyone had already figured that out. "What do we do now?"

Bulbo sighed, looked around at all the expectant dwarves, and said "Who's there?"

"You're dragging!" said the parrot.

"You're dragging who?" said Bulbo.

"You're dragging is dead!" said the parrot.

"What in the world is he talking about?" said Borin to Bulbo.

"He said "Your dragon is dead.""

"I don't get it," said Borin.

"Your dragon is dead," said the parrot again. "I saw him shot and killed as he destroyed Lake City. Awk!"

"What a stupid knock-knock joke!" said Fallin.

"Smog is dead, and Lake City destroyed?" said Borin. "This is the best day ever! The treasure is ours, and we don't have to pay for the food, lodgings or necessaries the Lake Citiziens sold us on credit! We're rich, and our creditors are dead! It's a dwarf's dream come true!" Borin broke into an impromptu victory dance on his pile of alternative-lifestyle jewelry.

"No, that's not what I said. Awk! The people of Lake City escaped with their Mayor."

"Oh," said Borin. He looked a little disappointed, but it passed. "Well, we're still rich, even after we eventually settle up with the Lake Citiziens. Just let them submit their invoices, wait for ninety days, and then we'll pay them. It's not like we actually have to split our treasure with them."

"Well, yes, you do have to split it with them," said the parrot. He was steadily becoming more and more articulate,

168

far more than anyone expected from a parrot. "Their sheriff killed the dragon, which they feel gives them a claim on the late Smog's estate. Some of it was theirs anyway, on deposit with SmithiBank. Also, they helped you when you were desperate. Finally, your adventure resulted in the destruction of their city. Awk!"

"Boo hoo!" said Borin. "I hate sob stories. Even so, we can buy them off with a percentage of the net proceeds and return to them whatever they have on deposit, and we'll still be rich."

"Not exactly," said the parrot. "They've asked the wood-elves for humanitarian aid, and a host of doctors, general contractors and warriors is headed this way from Murkywood. They'll want some of the treasure. They're SmithiBank depositors, too."

"Anyone else?" said Borin as he sighed heavily.

"So far, I've only told the spiders and the eagles. But you should also expect to hear from the rargs and the goblins. Oh, and I told Enron, too. That's about it.

"Awk!" he added, as an afterthought.

"There's going to be a run on the bank!" said Borin. "If they all come and ask to withdraw their principal, we'll be ruined. I suppose we could fortify the entrance and kill anyone who tries to close their account. Wretched bird, why have you done this?"

"I just wanted to feel important," said the parrot. "I had big news to share! I'm sorry. I didn't mean to upset anyone."

"Upset?" said Borin. "I'm furious! We came here to kill a dragon, not to fight all of Little Earth!"

"I said I was sorry."

"That won't bring home my treasure! Now what do I do?"

"I could go tell your cousin Dwayne in the Ironing Board Hills about Smog. Maybe he could send help. Awk!"

"Incredible!" said Borin. "You told all of Little Earth, but you didn't tell the dwarves?"

"I was pretty busy. How many times do you want me to apologize?"

"Just get going and tell Dwayne to get here ASAP with every warrior he has on the payroll. He should hire some extras as temps, too."

"I can do that, if you want. But I don't think you'll be able to fight your way out. I think making your depositors' funds available might work better. It would certainly be better customer service."

"Everyone's an expert on customer service," said Borin. "Thanks for your input, parrot, but you've done more than enough already. Just get word to Dwayne, will you?"

"Happy to help. Awk!" said the parrot as he flew out and off towards the Ironing Board Hills.

Borin thought of something he should have told the bird. "Blast! I forgot to mention wagons for the treasure! Why do I have to do all the thinking around here? And why isn't anyone barricading the entrance!"

"Oh no," thought Bulbo. "This is going to get worse before it gets better."

*   *   *

Work began, with no further help from Borin, on fortifying the main entrance. The dwarves piled desks, filing cabinets and credenzas into a haphazard barricade in the SmithiBank reception area. The whole thing had the feel of kids at home on a snow day, building a fort in the living room with folding chairs, couch cushions and blankets. They were having great fun, and they kept at it for days.

Bulbo kept busy thinking about food. He was experimenting with ways of making the *crap* snack bars more palatable.

"If only I had something to put on these pieces of *crap*. But there's nothing here. No peanut butter, no sour cream and onion dip, not even any hummus." His only success was a mixture of crushed *crap* and water, which the dwarves used to cement together their wall of office furniture.

There came a night when lights of a huge camp could be seen in the valley below the Mountain.

"I see them!" said Deali. "A host of wood-elves, and their guests, the militia from Lake City!"

"I saw them first," said Fallin.

"Break it up, you two," said Borin. "We've got a busy day tomorrow."

The next morning a handful of elves and militia set out from a large camp they had built during the night at the foot of the Mountain. They approached SmithiBank cautiously, like heavily armed secret shoppers.

Bufu climbed unsteadily onto a rotating desk chair at the top of the barricade and hailed them. "Welcome to Smithi Financial Solutions. I'm Bufu. How may I help you?"

The scouts were surprised. Service at the old SmithiBank had never been this friendly. Before they could speak up, Bufu tried some cross selling.

"Do you own your own home?" he asked. "This is a great time to consider an equity line of credit. Or how about a free checking account for your small business?"

The scouts' mood changed quickly at Bufu's presumptive sales approach. They spoke up.

"You didn't assess our needs before you made your sales pitch!" said an elf. "You didn't even try to build rapport with us! This is just like the old SmithiBank after all." They turned and walked off.

"You'll be back!" jeered Borin, who had been watching intently. "Where else can you go? To a credit union?"

Pleased with themselves, the dwarves struck up a song for the first time in weeks. Bulbo hoped it would be something he could hum afterward.

> *The king went under the mountain*
> *The dwarves went under the mountain*
> *A wobbit went to the mountain*
> *To see if Smog was dead*
>
> *To see if Smog was dead*
> *The king cut off his head*
> *They bravely went to the mountain*
> *And killed the dragon dead*

Their song appeared to please Borin, despite the reprise of the tedious Lake City melody. Bulbo was amazed at how quickly the dwarves had taken credit for the sacrifice, skill, and bravery of others.

The next morning a squad of wood-elves and lake men entered the lobby of the old SmithiBank. The elves bore their hockey sticks, and the lake men bore pitchforks and torches despite the broad daylight. They all brandished savings account passbooks. They serpentined their way through the velvet ropes that Deali had set up during the night. When they reached the barricade at the front of the line, Bufu hailed them again.

"Welcome to Smithi Financial Solutions. I'm Bufu. How may I help you?"

A tall man came forward. He chewed the end of a little cigar, wore a serape, and carried an ivory-handled longbow. He squinted at Bufu and said "Can I talk to your manager, please?"

"Let me see if he's available," said Bufu. He scrambled down off the barricade. The elves and men made small talk. They complained quietly to each other about the delay, and about how understaffed SmithiBank had become.

Borin appeared and climbed the barricade. He clung to the desk chair and called down "Hello, I'm Borin, the manager here. What seems to be the problem?"

"I have a question about my account balance," said the squinty-eyed customer.

"I see," said Borin. "What did you say your name was, sir?"

"I didn't say," said the man. "But to move things along, I will. My name is Bart, Bart The Bowman. I'm the sheriff of Lake City."

He held up his bow. "And this is a six and a half foot yew bow with a ninety-eight pound draw, the most powerful longbow in the world, and can put an arrow clean through—"

"Could you please get to the point, sir?" Borin said. "There's a lot of customers waiting." He had spent most of his life talking with angry depositors that wanted to kill him. This sort of thing didn't easily shake him.

"These folks would like to close their accounts," said Bart.

"I'm sorry to hear that," said Borin. He held up some papers. "We can get started on that right away. Just have each of your friends fill out one of these Lost And Abandoned Property Claim Forms and have it notarized. We'll review each claim and respond within forty-five days.

"Forty-five days?" said Bart. "Claim form? Notarized?"

"Yes. The dragon destroyed all our recordkeeping. But now that I've cut off his head, we can rush your claims through."

"You killed the dragon, did you?" Bart squinted even harder. Then he smiled. "Oh I get it! You're kidding! But you're upsetting my friends. These elves get the crazy idea you're laughing at them and they don't like being laughed at. Just apologize to them, as I know you will, and then we'll close our accounts. Pay them for the damage you caused in Murkywood, pay us for your food, lodging, and necessaries, and we'll be on our way."

"Apologize? Pay?" said Borin. "Never! Dwarves, pick up your bows!"

As the dwarves started looking around for their bows, Bart suddenly had an arrow nocked and his longbow drawn, with the arrow pointed at Borin. Borin couldn't help but notice how close he was to being dead.

"Dwarves! Belay that order!" he said. He turned back to Bart. "You realize that bank robbery is a serious offense."

"Like I said, I'm the sheriff here, and this isn't a bank robbery. I'm just encouraging you to expedite our payments."

"We will do no such thing!" said Borin. "I'll give you one more chance. Come back tomorrow, without your elf legbreakers, and you can fill out your paperwork in my office."

"No, Borin," said Bart. He put down his bow. "Instead, you let us know when you're ready to pay us what's ours. Until then, you can inventory the treasure and feast on all the *crap* we sold you. I'm told it's pretty good crumbled on a green salad. But you probably don't have any lettuce."

Bart and his group turned and started back to their camp.

"Wow!" said one of the militia to Bart. "I've never heard you talk to anyone that much without shooting!"

Borin had come down and resumed his search for the Delta Burkenstone. He failed to find it, of course, and his irritation at being besieged became anger. His anger gave way to misery during dinner.

"The dragon smell in here makes this *crap* taste especially bad," he said. "How dare the Lake Citiziens deny us our lettuce!"

"I wish I had a salad," said Fatso.

"Me too," said Bulbo. He stood up to brush off some crumbs, and hoped that no one would notice the Delta Burkenstone-shaped lump in his pants.

Chapter 16

IT TAKES A THIEF IN THE NIGHT

As the days passed, the *crap* tasted even worse. And despite the inventory the dwarves took of the treasure, the Delta Burkenstone remained mysteriously absent.

"That big, beautiful jewel belongs to me," Borin said to everyone at the morning meeting. "Anyone that finds it should immediately request the first spot on the agenda at our afternoon meeting to inform me. Anyone that fails to notify me of its discovery can expect to be personally coached." He shook an iridium-plated war-hammer at them.

Bulbo felt like Borin was eyeing him, that perhaps he suspected. So that night he took the Delta Burkenstone out of his corduroy pants and started using it as a pillow. He discovered that the 24-karat solid gold pillow he had been using previously was actually much softer than his new diamond one.

The old parrot visited, apparently to force his knock-knock jokes on a literally captive audience. But he also brought news.

"Dwayne is on his way," said the parrot. "He is hurrying from the Ironing Board Hills with five hundred dwarves, and they are very grim. I told them a few knock-knock jokes, but they just got grimmer. Awk!"

"No kidding," said Bulbo.

"But they'll have to fight past all the warriors outside to reach you," said the parrot. "Then what? Your treasure is bringing you nothing but trouble. It will be the death of you, even though the dragon is gone!"

"There's some irony for you, Borin," said Bulbo.

"Thanks, I noticed," said Borin. "But perhaps as winter sets in, and with my friends nearby, Bart will be more open to negotiation. Paperwork and delays may yet win the day!" He waved the war-hammer about as he returned to his hunt for the Burkenstone.

Bulbo knew that Borin had always been difficult to deal with, but now he was not only difficult, but also crazy and actively dangerous. Bulbo had to be the one to take action, or things would get much, much worse. As usual.

He waited until night fell, as was becoming his habit, and put the Delta Burkenstone back into his pants. Then he scrounged up some rope and climbed to the top of the barricade. Fatso was there, on watch.

"Cold enough for you?" said the dwarf. "I can't feel my fingers anymore."

"Yeah, the wind chill up here is brutal," said Bulbo. "Listen, Fatso, I can't sleep. Maybe I ate too much *crap* on toast at dinner, or maybe my gold pillow is too lumpy, but I'm wide awake. Let me switch my watch duty with you. My shift starts at midnight. You go and warm up for a while. Beefi has started a cheerful campfire with old bearer bonds. I'll come and get you at midnight, and maybe I'll be sleepy by then. Would you do that for me?"

"Are you kidding? I'd love to switch! Hey, what's with the rope?"

"Oh, this?" Bulbo held up the rope and tried to act casual. It was a large coil of velvet rope from the Smithi Financial Solutions lobby.

"Um, Borin told me I was in charge of brushing the dust out of the velvet," said Bulbo. "Can you believe that guy?"

"He's a piece of work, Borin is," said Fatso. "Look at the mess he's got us in! You heard what the parrot said. Thirteen dwarves against all of Little Earth! Another step forward in Borin's Parade Of Mistakes. I should have resigned as soon as he hired Pantsoff."

Fatso stopped in mid-complaint to catch his breath. "I'm sorry, Bulbo. I guess this siege is really getting to me. I'd give anything for a decent meal, or even some traditional dwarf cooking."

"Tell me about it," said Bulbo. "Go ahead and warm up, and I'll see you at midnight."

"Thanks, Bulbo. For a wobbit, you're all right."

Bulbo ignored the insensitive remark as he watched Fatso huff and puff his way down off the barricade. He waited for a few moments, and then tied one end of the velvet rope to an old conference table leg. Soon, Bulbo was doing some huffing and puffing of his own as he descended the steep outer wall of the barricade. He left the rope hanging, put on his ring, and invisibly scuttled towards the bright lights, wonderful cooking smells and raucous laughter of his besieger's camp.

"I can't believe I'm doing this," the wobbit said to himself as he crept along the Runny River. He found a spot where the river narrowed. He tried to use some decorative stepping stones to get across, but it's difficult to use stepping stones when one's feet are invisible. Like trying to tie someone's necktie when you're standing in front of them. At the halfway point he missed a step and went knee-deep into ice-cold water.

"Son of a—" he started to say, and then he went completely off-balance and sat down in the water up to his chest. The splash was loud for someone of his size, and though he sat still and quiet in the water, hoping for the best, a pair of elf guards approached.

"That splash sounded like a walleye," said one wood-elf. "Or maybe even a muskie! Early tomorrow let's come back to this spot with our tackle and some beers, eh? Criminy, what fishing!"

"Oh, don't be a dimbulb," said the other. "You thought that was a fish, eh? Look there, a wobbit-shaped hole in the water. The queer little creature Borin keeps as a servant!"

"Queer indeed!" snorted Bulbo as he stood up with a splash and removed his ring. It was even colder out of the water than in.

"I need a blanket, a fire, some dry clothes, a hot meal, a few stiff drinks," said Bulbo to the elves, "and then I need to see Sheriff Bart as quickly as possible!"

Two hours after deserting the dwarves, Bulbo found himself eating a huge barbecue turkey leg in front of a roaring fire, taking long swigs from a flask of brandy. The wood-elf catering was even better than Bulbo remembered from his time in Murkywood. There were no clothes available in his size, but his own clothes were almost dry thanks to the unusually hot elf-fire. As he waited, he was quite comfortable in a thick plaid bathrobe he had been loaned. Bart and the Elvenking were looking at Bulbo, waiting for him to stop eating long enough to explain himself. They had been waiting quite a while. With his mouth still full, Bulbo finally spoke up.

"I haven't had turkey this good in ages! And this brandy is starting to go to my head, so I'd better get right to the point.

"I'm not going to sell out the dwarves, not even to get out of that dragon-stinking, *crap*-eating, metal-pillowed hellhole. But with Borin calling all the shots, I doubt any of us would ever get out of there alive. And there's no way I'll ever be able to get my share of the treasure back to Wobbiton.

"I want this siege overwith, and I want an armed escort all the way home. With a cook and butler. To be outfitted and provisioned by the wood-elves," Bulbo said as he silently toasted the Elvenking. "I don't care about my share of the treasure, but I'd like to be put on your payroll, your highness. Perhaps as the Murkywood Lodge Goodwill Ambassador To Wobbiton. Some phony-baloney job with health insurance and a 401k."

"And what," said the Elvenking, "will you do for us in return, little feller?"

"I'll give you this bargaining chip," Bulbo said, and he flopped the massive Delta Burkenstone on the ground in front of him.

Bart and the King gazed at it silently. It was as if a transparent water balloon had been over-filled with club soda, and was reflecting light from an especially gaudy Christmas tree.

"This is the Delta Burkenstone, the key asset among all the SmithiBank corporate holdings. Borin lusts after it, and will offer you anything to get it.

"I thought you weren't going to sell out the dwarves," said Bart with dwarf-like grimness.

"Sheriff, please!" squeaked Bulbo. He coughed, cleared his throat, and then continued talking. "That's better. Sheriff, I just want to avoid bloodshed, and this gem is the only thing Borin will negotiate for. Make sure to get on the agenda to present your offer at tomorrow's early meeting. Borin's cousin, Dwayne, will be here soon with five hundred dwarf warriors. I'm told they're grim, as grim as you. And now, if you'll excuse me, I must be on my way back to SmithiBank."

"Well, by golly," said the Elvenking. "This is an eye-opener and no mistake. You're all right, Mr. Bunkins. But do you really want to go back to Borin and his gang, eh? They'll be hopping mad when they find out what you've been up to."

Bulbo thought for a moment. "Your highness, you make an excellent point. I think I will stay here!"

As Bulbo was being shown to his tent, he passed an old man whose dark cloak couldn't quite conceal his bushy moustache. His voice was familiar.

"I was right again!" the old man said. "Bulbo, my lad, I knew you'd be the perfect addition to Borin's project team, and here you are! You've saved the day, thanks to me!"

"Pantsoff?" said Bulbo, hoping he was mistaken.

"Of course it's me!" he said, throwing back his cloak. "Who else? Now listen carefully. You must return to SmithiBank and await my signal. You'll know what to do. Until then you'll be absolutely safe. I'll make sure that Borin never learns that you gave us the stone. Just keep your feet on the ground and your head in the stars. Act enthusiastic and you'll be enthusiastic! Give your full 110%." Pantsoff went on like this for some time, until Bulbo was hypnotized by the relentless positivism of Pantsoff's rap.

Confused about the "signal," but hoping that Pantsoff's advice would be good, just this once, Bulbo hurried back to the barricade. He climbed up the velvet rope, which was just as difficult as he remembered from gym class. After a few false starts he made it to the top. He untied the rope, woke Fatso, and went to bed. He tried to forget his troubles with happy thoughts of bacon and eggs, but he couldn't stop worrying. He kept thinking "I hope I don't regret listening to Pantsoff."

Chapter 17

BATTLE OF SIX OR SEVEN ARMIES

Bulbo woke within SmithiBank, thoroughly regretting that he had accepted Pantsoff's advice. In the clear light of day, he realized it was idiotic to have returned to the dwarf camp. Borin would certainly discover Bulbo's betrayal before dinner.

"I don't even know why I'm here," Bulbo thought. "Pantsoff never told me his reason, assuming there is one."

Everyone was delighted to have Borin's early meeting interrupted by the return of the Elvenking and Bart The Bowman. They had their respective retainers along, as well as a very familiar-looking old man in a cloak. He was carrying a Murkywood Lodge tote-bag.

"I wonder who that could be?" thought Bulbo, who was so frustrated that he was now being sarcastic with himself.

"Hey, good day there!" said the Elvenking. "Borin, are you ready to talk politely and intelligently?"

"Never!" cried Borin from the barricade. "Politeness is for losers! Intelligence is a cheap substitute for confidence! My mind will not be changed by facts or truth. Like I said yesterday, submit your paperwork and your claims will be carefully considered."

"Is there nothing that you would negotiate for, eh?"

"Negotiate?" said Borin. "What are you talking about? No!"

"Are you sure?"

"I said no! You have nothing to negotiate with!"

"What if we told you we had the Delta Burkenstone, eh?"

"Oh please!" said Borin. "Don't be ridiculous! I'd give anything for the Burkenstone, but that doesn't matter because you couldn't possibly have it!"

"What if we do have it?" said the Elvenking.

"But you don't!"

"We do!"

"You don't!"

This kind of discourse was common between elves and dwarves. The Elvenking gave in first, and offered proof.

"We do have it, don't you know. Here it is, Mr. Big Shot Oakmanfield!" He pulled it from the old man's tote-bag and held it forth, shiny and bulging from both hands.

Borin sputtered and stammered, too upset at first even to accuse or attack. He eventually got hold of himself and started yelling.

"How dare you! That seductive boulder belongs to SmithiBank! To me! Give it back this instant!"

"You betcha. We'll give it back just as soon as you settle all our claims. You owe me my savings!"

"No! My father and my father's father already explained it to you! It wasn't a savings account! You had an investment portfolio with us, which can lose value! Didn't you read your prospectus?"

"More paperwork, eh? Okay, Borin, we've got your plus-size gem waiting here for you. You'll be able to cover it with bristly kisses the moment you give us back what's ours."

"But it's my Burkenstone!" said Borin. He then stopped being angry, and became suspicious instead. "If you don't mind, just how did you get hold of it?"

"We didn't 'get hold of it,' we were given it," said the old man. To the surprise of the dwarves, he let his cloak drop away and revealed himself. He spread his arms dramatically.

Bulbo was distracted by the thought, "I'm glad he has clothes on under there."

The old man said "Ha-ha! It is I, Pantsoff!"

"I knew it!" cried Borin. "That's the last time I hire a project manager because he bought me a few drinks!"

"You're welcome!" said Pantsoff.

"Then let me ask you, Pantsoff, exactly who 'gave you' my beautiful Delta Burkenstone?"

"Bulbo gave it to us," said Pantsoff. "Oh, wait a minute—"

But it was too late. Borin shrieked with frustration and rage.

Bulbo shrieked, too. Then he started yelling "Pantsoff, you rat! You son-of-a—" but he said no more, because Borin had picked him up and grabbed him round the neck. He was squeezing Bulbo like he was trying to get toothpaste out of him.

"You miserable wobbit!" Borin said. "You undersized—consultant!"

"So that's it at last," thought Bulbo as he fought for air. "He could have called me any insulting name at all, a thief or a traitor, but he chose the 'short' insults."

"Put down that wobbit!" said Pantsoff. "He was only doing as I directed. Bulbo bringing me the Burkenstone was all part of my plan, one which will exceed your wildest expectations very soon. Now let him go!"

Borin released Bulbo. Despite the dizziness, Bulbo had enough sense to let Pantsoff take credit for the Burkenstone Heist, even though it was completely Bulbo's idea. Maybe later he would bring it up, when everything had worked out and Borin was appropriately grateful. But not now.

"This is a conspiracy," Borin muttered. "Everyone's against me." He looked down at Bulbo.

"Well? Explain yourself, you short, um, shorty!" Borin would have time to think up some better insults while Bulbo was talking.

"Borin, my contract states quite clearly that I get a one-fourteenth share of the net proceeds from killing Smog. I choose the Delta Burkenstone as my entire share."

"Nonsense!" said Borin. "We offered you nothing of the sort! Our standard contract for a consultant is a per diem plus the consultant's weight in gold. That's the reason we switched Fatso from contract work to salary."

"It's true," said Fatso. "I was making a fortune as a SmithiBank contractor."

183

"Perhaps," said Bulbo, "but that's not the deal you offered me." He reached into his First Class Mailshirt and pulled out the tattered contract he received back in Wobbiton. "Look at what it says right here." He pointed at the key clause.

Borin glanced at the contract, at Bulbo, at the Burkenstone, at Pantsoff, at the host of warriors, and finally at Bart and the Elvenking whom he addressed directly, after a heavy sigh.

"All right, fine. I'll personally release all of your deposits. I'll refund all lost investments. I'll pay all outstanding invoices and I'll deliver all remaining merchandise on order, paid or unpaid. I'll have it all waiting for you tomorrow morning, right where you're standing. Just give me my stone!

"Yup," said Bart. "You'll get it tomorrow, when we get our treasure." Borin turned red.

"Fine!" Borin said furiously, and turned to Bulbo. "Now beat it, you!"

Bulbo scrambled down the steep front of the barricade. He wasn't about to wait for a velvet rope.

The day passed, and the night, too, as is usually the case. Word came to the camped host that Dwayne's dwarves were due to arrive that day.

Arrive they did, and they were terrible to behold. Their helmets were of iron, as was their armor, their boots, and their cummerbunds. Even their brass knuckles were iron. They were armed with massive, iron-bound tire irons. Their faces were grim, probably because it's uncomfortable to march in an all-iron uniform. Their beards were grimly French braided, and were decorated with little iron ornaments, which slightly offset the grimness. They hurried towards the Mountain as fast as their short, iron-clothed legs could carry them. Bart The Bowman went out to meet them.

"Hold it right there," he said through his clenched teeth and small cigar. "Who are you, and where are you going?"

"I am Dwayne, and I am here to meet with Borin Oakmanfield. We will help the New Improved Smithi

Financial Solutions meet its recent hiring needs. I bring trainees and temps, to serve you better. Now make way!

Bart didn't see a trainee or temp among them. He saw five hundred veteran banker-warriors. They bore great rucksacks packed with enough Spam, canned lima beans and powdered eggs to withstand a long siege.

"Make way!" said Dwayne again.

"Nope," said Bart. "We were in line to see Borin first. As soon as we're done with our business, it'll be your turn. Until then, git."

Something in Bart's eyes told them he was grimmer than any dwarf. They muttered and harrumphed, and then retreated to set up a camp of their own. Bart returned to his camp, to await the Burkenstone exchange the next morning. That was exactly what Dwayne wanted.

Suddenly, the dwarves attacked. Somehow, five hundred short-legged, iron-bound warriors in plain sight had won the element of surprise.

More suddenly, a darkness came on with dreadful swiftness. It was still early in the day, not even lunchtime. The darkness came like a vast cloud of jet-black top hats. "Perhaps the battle will have to be cancelled, called on account of darkness!" thought Bulbo.

"Halt!" cried Pantsoff, who appeared more suddenly than the darkness or the dwarves. There he was in the middle of the impending battle, a place he normally avoided.

"The Goblins are upon you! Blog, son of the Gobfather of the Moisty Mountains is coming!"

"The Goblins?" said Dwayne. "What fool stirred them up? They never go to battle this far from the Moisty Mountains. And where's the Gobfather? Why is Blog here?"

"He might still be angry that I killed the Gobfather," said Pantsoff.

Dwarves, Elves and Men all suddenly were looking at Pantsoff. Every one of them wondered what he would say next.

"Really, though," Pantsoff said, backpedaling, "by 'I killed the Gobfather' I mean his death was the result of a team effort. I was barely involved. In fact, it was more of a regrettable accident. What's done is done, that's what I say.

The important thing to remember is that none of this was my fault."

He knew he had to distract them quickly so that they wouldn't mob him while waiting for the goblins.

"Hey!" Pantsoff said. "Look at that! Bats flying above Blog's army, like a sea of locusts. There are Rargs, too, lots of them, like a sea of, um—"

Everybody waited.

"—like a sea of marmots! We're in a tight spot! Quickly now, let's talk! It's time for one of my foolproof plans!"

And so began a battle that none had expected, originally called the Battle Of Six Armies. Later on, more armies would arrive. A more accurate count was made after the battle, and it was renamed. So far, though, the combatants were The Axis Of Evil, comprised of the 1) Goblins, 2) Rargs, and 3) Bats. On the other side were The Allies Of Goodness, specifically the 4) Men, 5) Elves, and 6) Dwarves.

The Moisty Mountain Goblins had sworn a vendetta against Pantsoff. Co-named in the vendetta were Borin, the other dwarves, Bulbo, and SmithiBank. Blog, the new Gobfather, sent word to the Five Goblin Families, and they had all "gone to the mattresses" together. They sought vengeance, and some of them also had old SmithiBank personal money orders they wanted to cash. When they heard about Smog's death, the promise of unclaimed merchandise that could be sold at a discount for pure profit made them march even faster.

As the Axis Of Evil drew near, Pantsoff benefited from the ancient hatred between elves and goblins. Elves hated goblins even more than they hated dwarves. The wood-elves were so eager to kill goblins that they and everyone else forgot that the battle was Pantsoff's fault.

Pantsoff desperately tried to come up with a battle plan. He killed time by forcing a few team-building exercises on the group. It worked. Elves, dwarves and men worked together to get the teambuilding over with. Eventually someone else came up with a plan. It was Dwayne, who

186

interrupted the "fall back into my arms" exercise to share a plan based on his knowledge of goblin strategy.

"A goblin mob this huge won't use the tactics you're used to," Dwayne said. "Instead of luring you into a tavern, stabbing your hand to the bar and then strangling you from behind, they'll probably use an approach like this." He started drawing in the ash and dirt with a stick.

"The goblin's classical attack formation is in the shape of a fighting Chimera,' he said as he drew. "First, bats will form the Chimera's Wings, flapping forward. We're expected the move in and meet them. But it's only a feint. The bats will retreat, and then change formation, returning as the Chimera's encircling Tentacles." No one said anything, but they were already confused.

"They will expect us to advance again, only to be pinned by rargs in their Curly-Cue Tail formation. Finally, the goblins that form the Chimera's Hooves, Tongue and Eye-Stalks will all close in to destroy any pockets of resistance." The drawing looked like the assembly instructions for a roll-top desk from Ikea.

Pantsoff's mind had started to wander at the words "They'll probably use an approach like this." As the scratchings in the ash started to blow away, he said "It looks complicated."

"Oh, it's incredibly complicated," said Dwayne. "And it hardly ever works. If we can just stay put as they maneuver back and forth, they'll eventually become confused and we can defeat them.

"Well, okay then!" said the Elvenking. "You heard the dwarf, eh? To your posts, everyone!"

As armies Four, Five and Six readied themselves, army Three attacked in their Wing formation. The bats fluttered around the heads of the elves, because they were the tallest. But the Murkywood elves knew too much about the great outdoors to panic. Soon the bats were driven off.

The rargs arrived next, in the Curly-Cue Tail formation. The Lake City Militia hurled leftover pork ribs and kielbasa into their midst, creating confusion and discord as the rargs snapped and snarled at each other.

187

The Hooves and Eye-Stalk formations, all made up of goblins, arrived last. They were eager to begin their flashy maneuvers and show off their two-handed battle-garrotes. All six armies had arrived, and the battle was officially underway.

Bulbo was terrified. He had put on his ring early in the battle to hide from the vengeful Borin. Then he only just managed to get out of the way of a mighty wood-elf charge. He cringed as their deadly curling stones whistled past.

Goblins dislike winter sports in general, so the barrage caused them to panic. They dropped their hair-trigger switchblades and ran. Their rarg accomplices attacked the wounded goblins that had been left behind, eating them as was their custom. The goblins were so demoralized that they too started to eat wounded goblins.

But some of the goblin elite, the "made" goblins, had scaled the Only Mountain and were attacking from above. They were throwing cinder blocks stolen from a nearby construction site. They would not be beaten as easily as Dwayne had thought.

The goblins assembled into a titanic battle-mob for a new onslaught. Fresh rargs, as yet unbloated by goblin-meat, had arrived. With them came the bodyguard of Blog. The bodyguard was made up of hemogoblins of tremendous size, carrying giant, wickedly-curved straight-razors.

Bulbo found a safe place and watched as Bart shot goblins with his long bow, killing one after another in rapid succession. Bart's speed and accuracy struck Bulbo as somehow supernatural. So too did the fact that Bart never ran out of arrows. Bulbo then noticed that despite Bart's amazing efforts, the goblins came closer and closer. As Bart lined up a difficult shot that would kill five goblins with one arrow, a cry rang out from the barricade.

"Get 'em, dwarves!" It was Borin! His battle cry wasn't clever, but it was heartfelt. Improvising battle cries and providing actual leadership weren't within Borin's comfort zone. Borin was better at managing through memos and subordinates. But there he was, personally involved in ordering his squad of relatives to attack.

The attacking SmithiBank board members were decked out in fabulous vintage armor from the SmithiBank vaults. They delighted many a doomed goblin with their funky, retro helmets and shields.

"To me! To me!" said Borin as he settled into his new role as field commander. "Dwarves, men, even you elves, to me!" Soon Borin had reassembled around him the great host of allies. They advanced as one, scattering goblins and rargs before them, shooing away the occasional bat. But when they reached the bodyguard of Blog, they could not pierce its ranks.

The hemogoblins, some of them so huge they could stand shoulder-high to an elf, drove off attack after attack, unafraid of elf hockey sticks or dwarf tire-irons. Doing all the attacking soon wore out the allies. Blog was thus able to reassemble a host of his own while the elves, men and dwarves stopped to catch their breath and rest their sword-arms. The hemogoblins were joined by rargs, bats and regular-sized goblins, as they prepared for the last, great assault.

The safe place from which Bulbo had observed the battle was now no longer safe, not even by battlefield standards. Ever the survivor, he tried to figure a way of switching sides one last time, but came up with nothing. He skulked towards the Elvenking to get as far as possible from Borin. He hoped to avoid dying by his vengeful hand. Pantsoff was there too, sitting on some dead goblins. He appeared to be deep in thought, either preparing a magic blast that would turn Blog into a pile of caramel corn, or composing some truly memorable last words. Bulbo wasn't sure which.

He considered taking out his Elf Army Knife and making a last stand of his own, but he couldn't decide on the right tool to open. "Perhaps the phillips-head screwdriver would be good against an armored foe? Or do goblins hold their armor together with straight screws? Or bolts? Oh drat, the knife will be visible in any event!

"Should I take the ring off to die in combat, as my ancestor Bullshitter Dork would have done? If I stay invisible, I still might be killed by a stray arrow. Or maybe

I'll be completely overlooked. I could invisibly poach off the goblins, just as I did with the wood-elves! Oh, who am I kidding? It's too late for that.

"It just seems a shame that we should have to die after going to all this trouble. On the other hand, we were incredibly lucky to make it this far. What a time! I suppose I shall miss the dwarves. Some of them, anyway. I never really liked Borin, but who did? Fatso was all right though, and so were Tori and Groin. The Elvenking was nice, too. And that Bart, killing Smog with a single arrow! And even good old Pantsoff. Shall I never hear another of his lies? Are we all to die for nothing?"

Bulbo's invisible farewell address to himself was interrupted when the black clouds that darkened the battlefield broke up as suddenly as they arrived, revealing a red sunset. Seeing this sudden glimmering gleam in the gloom, he glommed onto the Elvenking, hoping to stay protected and alive long enough to enjoy the view. Then he saw a sight that made his heart skip a beat, just as had happened to Fatso so many times. Bulbo saw eagles!

"Look!" he said to the Elvenking, who was confused by Bulbo's invisible grip around his knees and his disembodied voice. "Everybody! Look! The Eagles are coming!"

Everybody looked up, except Borin. Borin grabbed his ball-peen warhammer and started searching for Bulbo, following the sound of his voice. By listening carefully, Borin figured Bulbo's head must be just to the right of the Elvenking's boot top.

"The eagles!" said Bulbo once more, giving Borin a perfect shot from behind.

"Excuse me," Borin said to the Elvenking, who politely stepped aside. Borin smote Bulbo heavily on his invisible helm. Bulbo fell to the ground with a small crash, and he knew no more.

Chapter 18

THE LONG GOODBYES

"I knew 'No more!' was what I should have told the bartender," said Bulbo, "but I couldn't! It was Happy Hour!" Bulbo was just waking up, disoriented, on the deserted battlefield. It was early morning.

"Wait! This isn't the Ass-Dragon Inn! Where am I? Why does my head hurt?" Then reality hit him, like an angry dwarf with a ball-peen warhammer.

"The battle with the goblins! Now I remember. The eagles came to our rescue, but what happened then? Who won?" He saw one lonely figure, a Lake City Militiaman tossing dead goblins into an over-loaded wheelbarrow.

"You there!" Bulbo called. "You with the dead goblins! Who won the battle?"

The man looked toward Bulbo. "All right, who's hiding over there? I've got a long day of burying goblins ahead of me, so please don't make it worse with practical jokes. Show yourself!"

"What are you talking about?" said Bulbo. "I'm standing right here! Or are you insulting me because I'm short? Well, I may be shorter than every elf, man and dwarf in Little Earth, but I've learned a few things since I left my basement apartment in Wobbiton last spring. So look out, you stupid grunt! Mr. Bulbo Bunkins, Wobbit and Consultant, is about to kick your—oh, wait a minute."

Bulbo remembered he still had his ring on. He took it off, and appeared suddenly in front of the large, disgruntled warrior he had just threatened. The man stepped back, startled, but then put a hand on his sword.

191

"What did you say your name was?"

"Bunkins!" Thinking clearly now, Bulbo realized that he really didn't want to come to blows with a warrior twice his height. "I'm the famous Bulbo Bunkins! Come on, buddy! The only wobbit this side of the Hidden Valley! Maybe you know my good friend, the wizard Pantsoff?"

"Pantsoff?" said the warrior, insulted at the implication that he might know the wizard.

"Come with me, Bunkins. Borin Oakmanfield of SmithiBank wants to see you." The warrior dumped the dead goblins out of his wheelbarrow and told Bulbo to get in. To his credit, he didn't tell Bulbo to "hop in."

Bulbo looked into the wheelbarrow, considered walking due to its unhygienic appearance, looked at the warrior, regretted his "stupid grunt" remark, and then delicately climbed aboard.

"I've got to remember to wash my hands when we get to camp," thought Bulbo. "Or perhaps I'll wait until after I meet with Borin. There's no sense in cleaning up if he's going to kill me anyway." Then he tried to think of what he would say to Borin if the dwarf didn't immediately kill him. But he was greeted by somebody else when he arrived in camp.

"Bunkins, my lad!" It was Pantsoff, of course. He wore a gory bandage on his arm, but the blood seemed to have been applied to the bandage from the outside. "I'm so glad you're not dead! That means I win the pool. I knew you were lucky from the start."

Bulbo awkwardly got out of the wheelbarrow, which is difficult for anyone. He winced at his lower back pain, aggravated by a night of sleeping outdoors in the cold and damp on dead bodies.

"How's the sore back, old timer?" asked Pantsoff.

"Almost as sore as my head. Borin tried to kill me."

"And who can blame him? Hey, that reminds me, he asked to see you as soon as you got here. This way." He gestured freely with his "wounded" arm.

"This will only take a minute," he said holding open the tent flap. Bulbo glanced about desperately, saw no chance for escape, breathed deeply, and entered.

To Bulbo's surprise and great relief, Borin was lying down, severely wounded. His retro vintage armor was in tatters, and his ball-peen warhammer was dented. He did not leap up and kill Bulbo.

Borin reached out to him, and Bulbo flinched away. Then he realized he was not being attacked. Bulbo cautiously took his hand, awaiting some sort of deathbed curse or accusation.

"Mr. Bunkins, I know we've had our differences. I am still devastated that you betrayed me. You stole the one treasure I valued above all others. You were always late to my meetings. Still though, you are the best consultant I've ever worked with. It was wrong of me to try and kill you.

"I don't want to pass on to the halls, lobbies and vaults of my fathers without expressing to you my personal appreciation, and the thanks of all SmithiBank. My one regret is that I can't reward your good work with a bonus. I'd love to, but I can't. It's against our policy. And now, farewell!"

Bulbo walked out and found a secluded spot. There, whether you believe it or not, he wept until his eyes were red. He muttered to himself in a hoarse, halting voice, "That cheapskate! Smog was right! I deliver a mountain of treasure to him almost single-handed, but he can't come up with a bonus for me!"

He badmouthed the deceased Borin for a while longer, and then pulled himself together. "Well, he didn't try to kill me again, so that's good. And most of my bosses over the years would have loved to kill me, but they didn't have the nerve. Borin was one of a kind.

"So now what do I do? It looks like I could actually get home alive, but how? What will I do? I—Oh look, lunch!"

Bulbo ate. Meanwhile, I will tell you something of the events following Borin's attempt on the wobbit's life. The eagles had seen every move the goblins made, and they were happy to help destroy them. They wanted a quieter neighborhood, and the battle gave them the perfect opportunity to help get rid of their least favorite neighbors.

Even with the eagles joining the Battle of Six or Seven Armies as army number seven, the goblins still held a huge advantage of numbers. As quickly as the eagles knocked them off the cliffs, new goblins would be pushed forward by their *capos*.

At the last hour, Bjork himself appeared. (Since he came alone, he did not qualify as an eighth army.) He had assumed his huge swan shape, and was even huger than normal. And he was very mad.

His swan-honk was like the honking of a huge, angry motorist. He knocked rargs and goblins aside like a wobbit fighting his way to a free smorgasbord. He found the wounded Borin and his dwarves making their last stand. With one mighty wing, he scooped up Borin and took him to safety.

Swiftly he returned, even madder then before. His feathers turned away switchblade and razor alike as he smashed Blog's bodyguard with wings and beak. Then he knocked down Blog himself, and crushed him flat with a giant, webbed foot.

That was simply too much for the goblins, who dropped their weapons and ran. The bats left, too, and so did the rargs, not even stopping for one last bite of their fallen comrades. By the time Bulbo was delivered to the camp by wheelbarrow, the battle had been over for hours.

Once Bulbo finished his lunch, he stopped in at Borin's funeral. Just as planned, he arrived near the end. He signed the guest book and looked forward to the reception, his second lunch of the day.

Bulbo saw Bart laying the Delta Burkenstone on Borin's breast. Fallin asked Bart if he would say a few words.

Bart cleared his throat and spat on the ground. "Better late than never," he said, exceeding his limit by one.

Then the Elvenking stepped forward with Borin's sword, Orcbriss. It had been taken from Borin when he was held captive by the wood-elves. The Elvenking returned it to him now, sadly placing it at Borin's side. With the sword, the Burkenstone, some symbolic hunks of *crap* from Lake City and a farewell loaf of bread with honey from Bjork, you could barely see Borin.

You could still see the sword, and it is said that it always gleamed in the dark if foes approached. Ever after, a dwarf stood guard in Borin's darkened tomb, watching Orcbriss to see if it glowed. It was the most boring duty Dwayne could assign in the Lonely Mountain. But assign it he did, and other jobs, too. The dwarves, all of them somehow related, flocked to him to enjoy traditional dwarf nepotism. Of Borin's project team, ten remained. Wheeli and Deali had fallen defending him, for he was their mother's elder brother, otherwise known as their "uncle."

With Borin dead and gone, everyone agreed that the treasure left over after the payments to customers and creditors should be divided evenly among them. No one was sure who represented the estates of Wheeli and Deali. Instead of finding out, they simply split the treasure into tenths instead of thirteenths, which satisfied all the survivors. Borin, as far as anyone knew, had no family of his own, other than the typical "brother's youngest daughter" variety. He was lucky they let him keep the sword and Burkenstone.

The treasure that they divided was very great, and it included a great, mysterious surplus. They assumed it was primarily from the Goblin King Golfouting's deposits that were part of the bank's original formation. Fortunately, the Goblins were in no longer in any position to claim it.

The dwarves used this surplus to open the New Smithi Financial Solutions. The Only Mountain became their headquarters after all. The clean up was horrific, but they saved a fortune in marketing and advertising costs, thanks to the local good-will Dwayne had established. After settling all of Borin's debts with the Lake Citizens, he helped them to rebuild with a monumental Community Reinvestment Program. Following his refunding of the Elvenking's investment losses there was an unprecedented increase in wood-elf business and referrals. He loaned liberally at reasonable interest, and thanks to the stimulus provided by the death of Smog, Smithi Financial Solutions showed a profit sooner than anyone expected.

For his payment, Bulbo asked only for two small chests, one filled with silver, and the other with gold. Dwayne asked him about it.

"Bulbo, why don't you just take two chests of gold? You've probably heard that a chest of gold is much more valuable than a similar chest filled with silver, right? So why waste your time on silver?"

"Pantsoff suggested it," said Bulbo. "He said it would be a good way for me to diversify my portfolio. But I suppose you're right. Yes, make that two chests of gold, please."

The day came when he had to say goodbye to all his friends. At a testimonial breakfast at Smithi Financial Solutions, he ended his short speech with "Farewell Fallin! And farewell Crawlin! Farewell Rori, Gori, Tori, Loin, Groin, Beefi, and Bufu. Fatso, I think I shall miss you most of all. Farewell Borin Oakmanfield! May your bank never fail!" Bulbo turned and walked out.

Then he came back in to add, "Wheeli and Deali, farewell to you, too."

The dwarves stopped him, and then bowed low in their redecorated bank lobby. "Goodbye and good luck!" said Fallin. "If you ever visit, please remember that you have no remaining claims against SmithiBank. The two chests of gold represent our complete payment for your services."

"If you're ever in Wobbiton," Bulbo said, "be sure to make reservations at an inn. Maybe we can meet somewhere for coffee."

He turned away again and was joined by Pantsoff, who asked "Mind if I tag along?"

They accompanied the elves, who were glad to be returning to their lodge. The elves looked forward to a spring of joy and abundance, even as they began their winter of colds and flu. The dragon was dead and the goblins were overthrown. They were at peace, knowing that Evil had been cast out of Little Earth once and for all. At the time, Bulbo had no way of detecting any irony in their joy.

Bjork walked with Pantsoff and Bulbo, who were riding two Lake City ponies that Smog missed. Along the way, he shared his knowledge of the wilderness, like "Leaves of three, let it be. Soft and brown, put it down." He liked to make observations, like "Look, rainbow! Rainbows good!" or "Look, trailside litter! Litter bad!" or "Look, bunny rabbit!

196

Bunnies good!" Most of what he pointed out was "good." He seemed a little less excitable than when they first met.

When they reached Murkywood, Bulbo chose to go around it with Bjork rather than entering with the wood-elves. He had noticed the absence of giant spiders from the Battle Of Six Or Seven Armies. He suspected they might still be alive in force and holding a grudge. He patted Stink, all its blades folded and in his pocket, as they said goodbye to the elves.

Bulbo suffered many hardships and had many adventures on his way home, but none that were interesting enough to write in a book. The sight of Bjork kept most troublemakers away, and Pantsoff was providing less misdirection than usual.

By mid-winter they were back having breakfast after breakfast at Bjork's compound. Yuletide was pretty quiet: they hung stockings at the mantle, but exchanged no other gifts. In January, Bjork hunted down the last terrified local goblins and smashed them. There was a new peace, and the goblins never returned. Not to Bjork's neighborhood, anyway.

Pantsoff insisted that they freeload off Bjork until spring came. Then they packed all the bread and honey they could carry and said farewell. After that, Bulbo was never able to eat another continental breakfast.

Bulbo's adventure-loving Dorkish side was just about worn out, and his old Bunkins stodginess had never been stronger. "I can't wait to stretch out in my own recliner," he said.

Chapter 19

THE LAST LAUGH

It was on May the first that they found, after a lot of searching, the Hidden Valley. Bulbo was looking forward to ordering off the extensive menu at the Last Waffle House, and sleeping in a king size bed with a mint on the pillow.

Just as Bulbo expected, the elves were singing as they valet-parked the ponies, which were of regular size. The singing was the same as the last time they visited, just with different verses.

> *The dragon is wasted*
> *The goblins are murdered*
> *And now, you'll vacation*
> *With loins all ungirded*
> > *O! tri-lil-lil-lolly*
> > *You're back in our valley*
> > *Both Bulbo and Pantsoff*
> > *Alive, Alive-O!*
>
> *The world is much better*
> *The darkness is banished*
> *We'll have lovely weather*
> *Please try our club sandwich*
> > *O! tra-la-la-lally*
> > *You two seem so jolly*
> > *We're glad there's no dwarves with you*
> > *Singing "Heigh-ho"*

As their bags were brought to their rooms, Enron came to the front desk and greeted Bulbo and Pantsoff warmly. Because he wanted news.

"Let me treat the two of you to dinner!" said Enron. "Join me at my private table in our new tapas bar. We can eat right now! You two must be famished."

Pantsoff knew this might be a limited-time offer. Although he and Bulbo hadn't yet been to their rooms, Pantsoff accepted the invitation for both of them. Before they knew it, they were whisked to Enron's special booth in his new restaurant, Top Tapas Bar None. They drank pitcher after pitcher of sangria as Pantsoff recounted the entire adventure to Enron. Enron asked a few follow-up questions, and then lost interest.

Pantsoff started blathering to Bulbo about some of his recent exploits with Enron. He went on and on about all the important networking he did at the All-Wizard Annual Golf Outing he attended while the rest of Borin & Company were struggling through Murkywood. Bulbo had heard these anecdotes many times on the journey from Lake City, and while staying with Bjork.

"It was magnificent, Bulbo! Remember when I told you about the evil Neccomancer? Well, our golfing was rained out one day, so instead we attacked him in his dark tower. We cast him out! You should have seen me!"

"The two of you had quite a showdown," said Enron. "Too bad you weren't able to kill him."

"Not to worry," said Pantsoff. "After the beating he took, he's never coming back. Trust me!"

"Sorry to interrupt," said Bulbo, "but shouldn't we order our dinners? I'm getting tired of all these appetizers."

"Keep drinking, Bulbo," said Enron. "The appetizers are the dinner. You've really got to get out of Wobbiton more often."

So Pantsoff and Enron drank, and talked again about the Battle Of Six Or Seven Armies, and ate, and talked some more, and drank, and then when Bulbo thought they were finally done, Pantsoff ordered coffee. Bulbo was so incredibly bored that he deliberately went to sleep at the table.

Bulbo woke in his darkened suite. Elves were singing in the hallway, just outside his door.

The more we sing together

Together, together
The more we sing together
The happier you'll be

We're noisy on purpose
We're your wake-up service

The more we sing together
You'll wake up on time!

"Are you kidding me?" Bulbo said as he opened the door. "I didn't request a wake-up call!"

"Didn't you?" said one of the elves. "Oh wait, we're at the wrong room!" The elves went down the hall and sang again at another door.

"This certainly isn't the Murkywood Lodge!" said Bulbo. "The wood-elves would have at least given me a sincere apology and a coupon for a free breakfast."

"We're not wood elves, sir," the elves called back. "We're the other kind of elves, you know, just regular elves."

"No, I don't know," said Bulbo as he closed the door. "It must be like the difference between Dorks and Bunkinses." He ate some macadamia nuts out of the mini-bar and got back into bed until 11:00.

There were no more wake-up call errors, and the rest of their stay was relatively quiet. Every day, Bulbo pocketed some of those little bars of soap and little bottles of shampoo, which were normal size for a wobbit. He also had his Elf Army Knife professionally cleaned and reconditioned by the experts at the Swordatorium. It no longer had any Stink, but that was its name forever after. By the end of the week, he and Pantsoff felt well nourished and well rested. They checked out, thanked Enron, and were on their way.

It was a long journey, and without any adventures worth documenting. Spring slowly gave way to summer. "Are we there yet?" asked Bulbo as they rode.

"Not yet," said Pantsoff. "But we will be soon."

One day they passed the cave where they were almost eaten by Joe, Harry and Shirley, the three trolls.

"Those hideous monsters almost killed us," said Bulbo with a sigh. "Good times. Hey, there's the large, secret

'X' you left to mark our treasure! I don't suppose the dwarves will miss their shares. And how would they ever find out that we dug it up?"

"I like the way you think, Bunkins," said Pantsoff. They dug up the treasure and divided it between their annoyed ponies. Bulbo mopped his sweaty little face with a red silk handkerchief that bore an "E" monogram. He had borrowed it from Enron, and had "forgotten" to return it.

As all things must come to an end, Bulbo and Pantsoff finally ran out of adventures altogether. They had arrived at Wobbiton. As they rode toward Bug End, Bulbo sang quietly to himself.

> The show must go forever on
> > so if there's money to be made
> I'll once more put my mailshirt on
> > and kill a dragon again, someday
> Or else I'll send a relative
> > off to risk his limb and life
> To him my magic ring I'll give
> > and my magic Elf Army Knife
>
> He'll march all over Little Earth
> > Maybe he'll bring some friends along
> They'll sing some songs and make some mirth
> > And nothing possibly could go wrong
> This wobbit will recrown the king
> > And then sail off into the west
> He'll put away the magic ring
> > Tucking it back in his little vest

Pantsoff looked startled. "My dear Bulbo!" he said. "That was unexpected. I never knew you were a singer-songwriter. You are not the wobbit that you were."

"Nope!" said Bulbo. "Now I write my own songs, I'm in great shape, I'm incredibly wealthy, and I've killed giant spiders with a pocket knife."

And so they passed the Gristle Mill and the Best Uttermost Western Motel, and came right back to Bulbo's aluminum screen door.

"Hey! What's going on?" he cried. Wobbits were crowded around his door, smoking, spitting and loudly playing their nose flutes.

It was then that he noticed a large sign facing the street, stating that on June the Twenty-Second, Messrs. Dewey, Cheatham and Howe were to sell by auction the personal property of Mr. Bulbo Bunkins of Bug-End, Wobbiton. Sale at 10:00 sharp. It was now noon and the sale only just beginning.

"Typical," said Bulbo. "These provincial wobbits and their slow-paced lifestyle. They have no idea who they're dealing with! I'm a busy and important wobbit!"

Loudly he called out, "Who's in charge here?"

"I am!" said a familiar voice. It was Virginia, Bulbo's landlady. "Long time no see, Bunkins!"

"Virginia, what's going on? You can't sell all my stuff!"

"Sure I can! You owe me twelve months of back rent! I would have had you evicted a lot sooner, but Wobbiton law makes that almost impossible. I've been in court since November trying to clear you out!"

"But didn't you get my note? I wrote a note for you to sub-let the place while I was gone. I gave it to Pantsoff with my key, and he said he gave it to you!"

"I knew I forgot something," said Pantsoff.

"You idiot!" said Bulbo. "Now what do I do? What about my stuff?"

"I had a feeling I'd end up with some of Smog's treasure," said Virginia. "You've got deep pockets now, Bunkins, so start paying."

He immediately paid Virginia her back rent, plus damages, plus some goodwill money, plus the first of many small personal gratuities.

Then Pantsoff and Bulbo spent the afternoon buying back Bulbo's belongings. By dinnertime Bulbo's recliner was back in its traditional spot, and Bulbo's rootball card collection had been bought back from his cousin, Earlobia Snackbag-Bunkins. He had to pay her the "mint-condition" price for a "good condition" collection, but it was his again. The Snackbag-Bunkinses forever begrudged Bulbo for "taking back" what was to have been the primary investment for their retirement.

Indeed Bulbo found that he had lost more than a recliner and some investment quality collectibles—he had lost his reputation. It is true that he became a Gold Club Member of the Hidden Valley Ranch, and he was honored by dwarves, wizards, elves, eagles and any giant swans that passed through town, but he had changed. He was no longer a bored, cheap, flabby loser. He was now thought of by all as "queer," but not in the way that the Dork family was thought of as queer. More of an unpredictable, dangerous sort of queer. He was no longer picked on, he was politely avoided.

Since he was rich, he didn't care what anyone thought. He developed a lot of expensive tastes and interests, but he kept them secret. Outwardly, he led a quiet life. His Elf Army Knife he used at home to remove corks and open cans. His First Class Mailshirt he loaned to a museum that he built as a tax write-off. His gold he spent mostly in secret on his frequent out-of-town junkets, but he spread a lot of it around in Wobbiton to avoid being hassled. His magic ring he kept secret and safe, although he couldn't stop thinking about it. Ever. Whenever he left home without it, he got a nagging, uneasy feeling. The same feeling you or I get when we're halfway to the airport and we wonder if we left the front door unlocked.

He took to writing children's books, as celebrities often do. His neighbors were incredibly jealous and though many shook their heads and said "Lucky Bunkins!" he remained happy until the end of his days. And those days lasted an unnaturally long time.

One autumn evening years afterward, there was a rattly knock on Bulbo's screen door. It was Pantsoff, who invited himself in and mixed up a shaker of martinis. Fallin came in with him.

"Come in!" said Bulbo, after the fact. Fallin noticed, with his sharp eyes, that Bulbo had redecorated with the obvious help of an interior designer. Bulbo noticed that Fallin's beard had been expertly conditioned and braided.

Fallin boasted to Bulbo that Smithi Financial Solutions was bigger and more prosperous than ever. They had branches everywhere. In Wobbiton, there was one intersection that had a Smithi branch on each corner. He said that Lake City had shared in their prosperity. Even though Sheriff Bart had the Mayor arrested for embezzlement, the Lake Citiziens ever after thought of him, felon or not, as the Mayor Who Built The New Lake City.

"So he left a great legacy, as he had hoped!" said Bulbo.

"Of course!" said Pantsoff. "And all because I insisted on Borin hiring you as a contractor."

"Are you kidding?" said Fallin. "All because of Bulbo? Bulbo, no offense, but you're just one stupid, weak, frightened, clumsy little fellow in the wide world. After all, the whole adventure succeeded thanks to Borin!"

"Oh, please!" said Pantsoff. "Borin couldn't comb his beard on his own. He never could have recovered the treasure without Bulbo. You remember! The guy was an idiot!"

"He's right," said Bulbo. "No swords, no plan to kill the dragon, no idea how to enter the mountain. Really, Borin was a moron!"

"Do you mind? He was my cousin! And he's dead!"

"Thank goodness!" said Bulbo laughing, and handed him the martini shaker.

If you are interested in Wobbits, you will learn a lot more about them in <u>The CEO Of The Rings</u>:
1. SUPERFRIENDS OF THE RING
2. GOL-GOL'S REVENGE
3. RETURN OF THE SON OF THE KING STRIKES BACK FULL THROTTLE

Acknowledgements

Thanks to James Finn Garner for the mighty work he did getting The Wobbit formatted for Kindle and in front of the world, and for being my publishing sensei.

Thanks to Carsten Polzin at Piper Verlag for finding my book on the internet, publishing it, and asking me for a second book.

Thanks to Benjamin Chandler for his extensive comments, many meetings, and brilliant drawings, despite the fact that his only reference point for The Hobbit was the Rankin-Bass cartoon.

Thanks to Jean Kloth for her razor-sharp editing and writing suggestions, even though she has no interest whatsoever in Tolkien's writings.

Thanks to Rick Kirk for his Tolkien insights, his comedy-writing suggestions, and his entertaining read-throughs.

Thanks to John O'Neill, my biggest fan in Scotland, for actually reading the book and then visiting the website to tell me how much he enjoyed it.

Thanks to Stephen Lynch for championing my book on his excellent website, thehobbitmovie.co.uk.

Thanks to my friends at HobbitMovieForum.com (Forumshire): Ringdrotten, Petty Tyrant, Eldorion, Odo Banks, Orwell, Gandalf's Beard and all the others who provided endless support when most online forums regarded my excerpt postings as spam (when they are in fact *entertaining* spam).

Thanks to Zoe Erickson for her reluctant but charming artwork.

205

Thanks to Bill at Sign Express, Oak Park, Illinois, for his encouragement and promotional suggestions, especially the Ironic Bookmark.

Thanks to Maureen and the rest of the crew at the Forest Park, Illinois Starbucks for all of the refills.

Thanks to Becca Erickson for providing the real-life inspiration for The Incredible Bjork.

About the Author

Paul Erickson's mission in life is to be the world's foremost Tolkien parodist. (He's a bit of an underachiever.) Erickson was born in 1959, and has lived his entire life in the Chicago suburb of Oak Park. He read The Hobbit in 7th grade, and then read Bored Of The Rings that summer. He spent most of his high school years playing Dungeons & Dragons and attempting to read The Lord Of The Rings. In college he worked at the Bristol Renaissance Faire, wearing tights and selling love songs. After earning a BA in Philosophy he went into banking.

In the late eighties he performed song parodies in comedy clubs with ace guitarist Steve Ginensky. In the nineties he parodied slam poetry as part of Team Chicago, winning the 1991 Poetry Slam Nationals. In 2009 his banking career was cut short when his employer went out of business. Fortunately, by that time he had finished reading The Lord Of The Rings. While in line at the unemployment office, he realized no one in the US had ever published a parody of The Hobbit.

He went to Starbucks with his MacBook and got to work, combining all his nerd knowledge of Middle-Earth with his one real skill: writing parodies. In 2011, with the help of bestselling humorist James Finn Garner (Politically Correct Bedtime Stories) he published The Wobbit A Parody on Kindle.

The Wobbit A Parody was published as a German paperback in 2012 by Piper Verlag. They will be publishing Erickson's next parody, The Superfriends Of The Ring in October, 2013

You can visit Paul at TheWobbitAParody.com.